CW01184085

SHE WHO DARED

SHE WHO DARED

COVERT OPERATIONS IN NORTHERN IRELAND WITH THE SAS

by

Jackie George
with
Susan Ottaway

LEO COOPER

First published in Great Britain in 1999 by
LEO COOPER
an imprint of
Pen & Sword Books Ltd
47 Church Street
Barnsley
South Yorkshire
S70 2AS

© Jackie George, Susan Ottaway, 1999

ISBN 0 85052 686 8

A catalogue record for this book is
available from the British Library

Typeset in 12/13pt Bembo by
Phoenix Typesetting, Ilkley, West Yorkshire
Printed and bound in Great Britain by
Mackays of Chatham plc, Chatham, Kent

Owing to the sensitivity of the contents of this book, the manuscript was submitted to the Ministry of Defence prior to publication. At their request some changes were made to the text – including altering the names of individuals and places – in order to protect the work of the unit in their fight against terrorism.

GLOSSARY

14 INT SY COY (NI)	14 Intelligence Security Company (Northern Ireland)
8 Sigs	8 Signal Regiment
9mm	Bullet or Pistol
ASU	Active Service Unit
BASHA	living quarters
BEAST	verb, meaning to exercise
CO	Commanding Officer
COMMCEN	Communications Centre
CQB	Close Quarter Battle
CTR	Close Target Recce
DET	Detachment
DOP	Drop-off Point
DS	Directing Staff
DTG	Data Telegraphist
FOXTROT	to go walkabout
G3	Rifle
GREEN ARMY	Regular army
HK53	Heckler Koch 53 model Machine Gun
HMSU	Headquarters Mobile Support Unit (RUC backup for 14 Int Sy Coy)
IRA	Irish Republican Army
MM	Military Medal
MoD	Ministry of Defence
MP5K	Machine Pistol 5-Kurtz

NBC	Nuclear, Biological and Chemical drills
NCO	Non-Commissioned Officer
ND	Negligent Discharge
OP	Observation Post
PARA	Paratrooper
POW	Prisoner of War
PTI	Physical Training Instructor
QGM	Queen's Gallantry Medal
RUC	Royal Ulster Constabulary
SIB	Special Investigation Branch
SLR	Self-loading Rifle
SMG	Submachine Gun
WRAC	Women's Royal Army Corps
UDR	Ulster Defence Regiment

PROLOGUE

'What the . . . ,' Kevin began to speak and the tone of his voice made me look up. By the light of our headlamps I could see dark figures scuttling into the hedgerow. Ahead loomed a large dark shape. Kevin hit the brakes and my HK53 fell down and banged against my leg as he fought to control the nose-heavy car. I grabbed the stock as we skidded sideways and came to a stop, half on the grass verge. My pistol and the spare magazines dug into my back as I was hurled back into my seat. Then, because I was not wearing a seatbelt, I bounced forward again banging my head on the dashboard. Suddenly the car doors were opened and arms reached in, pulling me out of my seat and into the darkness. My head was spinning and I was losing my grip on the HK53. I could hear voices and one, with a strong Irish accent, shouted, 'She's got a gun.'

Someone pushed me to the ground and forced my face into the wet grass of the verge. I could smell the damp earth but was being held so tightly that I was unable to move. I was searched and my pistol was found. I tried to get up but only succeeded in raising my head and was kicked in the face by a man wearing heavy black boots. Once more I heard the Irish voice, this time shouting, 'Get down, bitch!'

I had never been so frightened in my life as I was at that moment. My heart was pounding and my breathing uneven. I was sure that Kevin and I were going to die and no one even knew that we were in trouble. The whole situation had developed so quickly that there had been no chance to call on the radio and, because we had left in such a hurry and were so far ahead of the others, we might be dead before anyone reached us. I could hear the car being ransacked and then there were delighted shouts as they discovered Kevin's G3 rifle on the back seat. This was followed by the sound of Kevin's groans as they began kicking him.

I started to struggle and managed to free one arm. As I raised myself to my knees a bright light was shone into my face and I was instructed to stay still. I could see dark figures coming towards me and with my last ounce of strength I shouted at them, 'Security forces, you bastards.' It was a stupid thing to say but somehow it made me feel better.

INTRODUCTION

Many people believe that the problems in Northern Ireland began on 5 October, 1968, with the Civil Rights march in Derry. The march had been banned by the Home Affairs Minister, William Craig, on 3 October, as there were fears that it would clash with the Apprentice Boys' parade that was planned for the same time. The march went ahead despite the ban.

It was a small demonstration, attended by only a few hundred people protesting about discrimination in housing and employment. It was quite peaceful until the police tried to break up the crowd, whereupon rioting, which lasted for two days, began.

Although it is true that the modern troubles did begin with this march, the real problems in Ireland go back hundreds of years.

When I first went to Northern Ireland I was curious about the cause of the troubles. The Army gave us plenty of training to enable us to carry out our covert duties, but no mention was made of the history that had created the need for an army presence. I wanted to know what it was that had led to such bitterness and hatred between the two Christian communities in this small country.

In 1170 a small party of Normans arrived at Baginbun on the south-west tip of County Wexford. They were the troops of the Earl of Pembroke, who was known as Strongbow, and had been invited to Ireland by the King of Leinster, Dermot Macmurrough, to help him with the fight he was having with his High King. As a reward for his help Strongbow was given Macmurrough's daughter in marriage and when Macmurrough died, Strongbow became King of Leinster himself. Back in England the King,

Henry II, was worried that Strongbow was trying to become too powerful and sent a force to put him in his place, thus establishing an English presence in Ireland.

Dislike of English rule in Ireland united some of the traditionally antagonistic groups and they fought against anything English, including conversion to Protestantism at the time of the Reformation of the Church. The country remained fiercely Catholic, although when English officials and settlers arrived a small Protestant group began to grow. The Protestants swore allegiance to the English crown whilst the Catholics longed to be their own masters once more. Because the Protestants remained loyal subjects they were given the most fertile land and the best conditions in which to live. As the years passed the unrest between the two groups began to grow, fuelled by the unfairness of their treatment.

In 1688 thirteen Protestant apprentice boys prevented the Catholic soldiers of King James II taking over the garrison in Londonderry. Two years later, in 1690, William of Orange defeated James II at the Battle of the Boyne. These two events have been commemorated ever since by the marches of the Protestant Orangemen and the animosity between the Protestants and Catholics has never been resolved.

In 1921 the Anglo-Irish Treaty was signed and the Irish Free State was created. It was to be a free country with its own armed services and its own government, while remaining a member of the British Commonwealth. Sovereign powers over the whole of Ireland were given to the Irish signatories of the Treaty but these powers were suspended for one month in the six counties of Ulster. This suspension allowed the counties to decide whether or not they wished to opt out of membership of the Free State and remain part of Britain. In this eventuality the boundaries between the two countries were to be reviewed and adjusted according to the wishes of the population. Tyrone and Fermanagh both had very large Catholic populations, but, in spite of this, they remained in the province of Ulster, which continued to be part of Britain. Eventually, in 1949, the Free State became the Republic of Ireland, severing all ties with Britain and the Commonwealth.

The Catholics of Ulster remained underdogs. Although they were in the majority in many areas, their representation in local government remained much less than that of the Protestants. In some areas the boundaries were redrawn ensuring that Protestant minorities could elect more councillors in the local elections than the Catholic majority. This inequality was also reflected in other areas such as housing and employment.

Whilst I cannot condone the atrocities committed by either the Republican terrorist groups or their Protestant equivalent, I can understand why Catholics feel anger and frustration at the discrimination they have suffered over the years at the hands of the Protestants. If they had been treated a little more fairly perhaps they might all have learned to live in peace with each other. Had that happened I would not have had a story to tell.

CHAPTER ONE

My parents were working class people and came from the same industrial town in the Midlands. They met during the war, when they were both employed by a company that supplied armoured vehicles. Mum worked as a clerk. Both she and her elder sister were very bright but in those days the opportunities for women were scarce. If she had had the chances that are available to women today, I am sure that Mum would have been a high-flyer. Dad, on the other hand, was never very ambitious. He worked as a labourer on the railway and later found himself a job at a local textile factory. As long as he had his motorbike, his pigeons and the time to go fishing he was happy. Dad was the oldest of three brothers. He lived in a two up, two down, terraced house in the rough end of town. I can remember the area; row upon row of dismal, red-brick terraced houses, blackened from the smoke of long silent factories. There was no bathroom and a tin bath was all they had for bathing. The whole family shared the water; Granddad first, followed by Dad and so on until they had all had a dip. Dad's mother ruled the roost in that household. She insisted on knowing everyone's business. Her lads could not sneeze without her permission. When Mum and Dad married, after a long courtship, it was Grandma who insisted that they live with her and Granddad, and Dad's younger brothers. It was hardly an ideal situation.

Mum, being so much more ambitious than Dad, pushed him to put their names down on the list for a council house and by the mid-1950s they were fortunate to be allocated a three-bedroom house on a large estate two miles out of town. The garden was big enough for Dad to have a pigeon loft and there was a brick outhouse for his motorbike.

During the first years of the marriage Mum had two miscarriages. Both she and Dad wanted children but had almost become resigned to the fact that they would never be parents when, after ten years of marriage, Mum became pregnant again. This time all went well and I was born, at four-fifteen pm on a Sunday afternoon in spring. Mum and Dad were overjoyed; for them life at last seemed complete. But the happiness, for which they had waited so long, was abruptly destroyed early one October morning when I was just six months old.

Dad always rode his beloved Triumph motorbike to work. That morning as he made his way down the road a pedestrian stepped out in front of him. Dad swerved to avoid him and crashed into a wall, suffering severe head injuries. He never regained consciousness and died later that day.

Suddenly Mum was alone with a small baby and a house to maintain. She had no job and no income. Dad's family was no help at all. Granddad only had time for his pigeons and the pub and Dad's death reduced Grandma to a bag of nerves. Fortunately Mum's sister, Hazel, took charge of the situation and within a few days of Dad's death moved in with us. Hazel had once been a captain in the Territorial Army and subsequently worked with them as an administrator. She spoke with a refined accent. Mum told me this was because she had been an officer. At the time she came to live with us she was single but was courting a chap called Bob who owned a garage. I remember he was always turning up at the house in a variety of different cars. Hazel was very chatty and confident. Mum was much more reserved but she was kind and patient and had a tremendous sense of humour.

I grew up in an all-female household and for the first six years of my life the only male influence I had was that of Granddad and Bob. Dad was hardly ever mentioned, except by Grandma. She was always telling me how much I looked like him and how proud he would have been of me for looking after Mum. I had no memory of him at all and thought it quite normal to grow up this way.

Sometimes Grandma took me to one of the pubs in the street where she and Granddad lived, thinking that it would be a great treat for me. I hated it. The atmosphere was so smoky that you could almost cut it with a knife. The women sat in the snug, their hair in pink rollers hidden under scarves and cigarettes dangling from their top lips as they gossiped. They spent hours discussing their neighbours' business. While the women talked, the men disappeared into the bar, to play dominoes or discuss the next pigeon race. Occasionally there was trouble; glasses smashed; chairs scraped across the wooden floor and the women stopped talking, craning their heads to see over the bar. They would listen to the raised voices and watch as the landlord threw the trouble-maker out of the bar. Once the excitement was over the women would shake their heads and continue gossiping as if nothing had happened. I sat there miserably waiting for Mum to come and collect me and take me home.

We lived in the middle of the estate and the green was opposite our house. I spent hours there playing football on what seemed to me to be a vast expanse of grass. I used to play with the boy from next door. Alan was a couple of years older than I was and I often went round to his house to play with his Scalextric. I hardly ever played with girls until I was five years old and went to school.

I was really excited when the time came for me to start school and on the first day Mum took me up to the school gates. I had never seen her cry before but as I went in she stood there sobbing. I was more interested in joining the game of football that was going on in the playground. This was the first time in my life that I had come into contact with children of my own age and I was painfully shy. I found it very difficult to settle and make friends, especially with the girls who wanted to sit and play with their dolls. When I did make friends it was with the boys who played the games that I liked to play.

I soon realized that I was the only child in my class who did not have a father. Single-parent families were not the norm in the mid-sixties and I did not want to appear different from my classmates. I was mortified when, one day, our teacher asked us all to tell the class what work our daddies did. I lied. I said that my Dad was an engineer and that he worked away from home. I carried on lying about my father for over a year and only stopped when Mum found out what I had been telling everyone. One day she was having a conversation with one of the other parents, who innocently mentioned how difficult it must be for her to cope with my father being away such a lot. Mum was horrified that I had been lying. She made me sit down and told me that I must not be ashamed of not having a father. I was angry. I just wanted to be like my classmates and wanted to know why my Dad was dead. Mum sent me to my bedroom. I knew that I had upset her because I could hear her crying. Later that day when Hazel came home from work she told me off about lying and I was confined to my bedroom for the rest of the evening.

At school I was like most of the other children, eagerly waiting for playtime. The minute the bell sounded we would rush out to the playground. There was always someone who had a football or an old tennis ball that we could kick about. I still did not want to play games with the girls; I was no good at them anyway. I preferred to play Cowboys and Indians with the boys. There were always arguments about which of us would be Indians. Everyone wanted to be a Cowboy as they always won. Sometimes we would play at being in the army. We would clasp our hands together and stretch out our arms, pretending to be tanks. The playground resounded to the noise of pretend machine guns which we 'fired' at each other.

It was around this time that I became interested in the army. Hazel's stories of soldiers on exercise and her tales of parties in the Mess were a big influence on me. It all sounded very exciting. Mum's father would sometimes tell me about his experiences in the Great War. He had been an engineer and, although he had suffered like everyone else with the terrible conditions, he had survived the war without injury. My grandmother's twin brother, Arthur, had also fought. He had joined his local regiment under age, after lying about his date of birth. He fought at Arras and was killed during the battle. He has no known grave. My grandmother was so proud of him. I remember her telling me how he had died for his King and country.

When I was seven years old Mum decided to move house. The court had finally released some money as compensation for Dad's death and Mum wanted to use it as a deposit for a semi-detached house that she had seen. The price was just over one thousand pounds and Mum was sure that if she got herself a part-time job she would be able to afford to buy it. I was about to start junior school, which would make it easier for Mum to get a job. The new house also had the advantage of being closer to Mum's parents.

Bob took us in his car to look at the house. The vendor was the DIY man from hell. It took Mum years to put right his mistakes. I can remember being horrified at the man's terrible taste. He had painted all the walls bright blue and the skirting board orange. He did, however, have a rather good Thunderbird collection and he promised that he would leave it for me when he moved. Mum paid the deposit and became a house owner at last. When we moved, Hazel found herself a flat two miles from our new house.

I started at my new junior school and began to do well. In my free time I joined a gang. It was small, only three members including me, with another couple of kids who hung around hoping to join. Our leader was a boy called Steve who was clever. I was the second in command and was followed by Ian, who was not very bright. Every Saturday morning we would go to the local toyshop and spend all our pocket money on Airfix kits and toy soldiers, which we would take back to one of our homes. We would spend hours trying to make sense of the instructions for building Lancaster bombers and other aircraft, but we always argued and never managed to finish any of our models. Then we would turn our attention to the soldiers. Steve and I always bought British soldiers, but we needed some Germans against whom we could fight. Poor Ian was always bullied into spending his money on the German soldiers so that we could re-enact some of the world's greatest battles.

We often played at the bottom of my garden where we made

an underground den. We played there quite happily until it collapsed after a heavy storm. Then we dug a trench in which we could kneel to conduct our battles. Finally we would set up all our soldiers and throw stones at them. Twenty-five years later Mum still occasionally finds a soldier while she is planting out her vegetables.

While I was at junior school Mum met a chap called Ron. He was ten years older than she was and owned a shop in another part of town. I could not understand why Ron kept coming to our house. Mum explained to me that she needed to have a friend. This confused me even more as I had always thought that I was her friend. Why did she want him when she had me? Ron tried to make friends with me but I would not let him. I could not bear him to come anywhere near me.

Sometimes Grandma would come over to our house in the evening to look after me while Mum went out with Ron. I hated it because she did not come home until after I had gone to bed. I would lie awake upstairs waiting for them to return and then listening as they laughed together. I was so jealous I could hardly bear it. One night I heard them come in and decided to sneak downstairs to see what they were doing. As I peeped through the half-open door I was horrified to find that they were kissing. I was filled with jealousy and anger and wanted to rush into the room and pull them apart. I could not understand how my mother could do this. I had always thought that she loved my Dad's memory. I wanted to punch Ron; instead I began to rebel. Whenever the opportunity arose, I would be rude to Ron. With the help of a friend I even damaged his car when he parked it outside our house. He was furious and, although he suspected that it was me who had done it, he could not prove anything.

In spite of my open hostility Mum continued to see Ron. He never lived with us but spent most evenings at our house. Sometimes he and Mum would go away for a short break and while they were away I was sent to stay with Hazel. She had married Bob and they had moved to a house in the country. It was during one of these visits that I discovered I was not alone in my dislike of Ron. Although he was always polite to my family, they were not impressed with him. He and Bob shared a passion for fishing but never got along well enough to go out together. Dad's side of the family was in complete agreement with me. Grandma made it very plain that Ron would never be as good as her son.

I began to keep a diary. Every day I wrote something unpleasant about Ron. I used terrible language to describe how I felt about his relationship with my mother. One day when I got home from school I was surprised to find that Mum was already there. One look at her face and I knew that something was wrong. She was furious with me. In her hand she held my diary and I at once realized that she had read it. I had never seen her so angry as, red-faced, she read out loud the obscenities I had written about her and Ron. Finally she flung the book at me and told me to go to my room to pack my things. I was stunned by the strength of her anger and expected a thrashing. I tried to apologize but Mum would not listen and pushed me aside. Ron stayed away after that and eventually Mum and I managed to get our lives back on an even keel. Although I had only wanted to save her from this man all I had done was cause trouble for everyone and when they parted soon afterwards I felt no pleasure or sense of victory. Mum told me that they had ended their relationship because she did not want to get married again but it did not make me feel any better. Memories of my early years are all clouded by my bad behaviour, both at home and at school.

When the time came for me to leave my junior school I went to the local comprehensive and became one of the first generation of comprehensive kids. My friends Steve and Ian went to the same school but our friendship did not last. Steve was put into the top class, I was in the middle and poor Ian ended up in the class for children with special needs.

I began to make friends with some other girls. They were not like the girls I had known at junior school. These were rebellious and I quickly joined their group. I had to be one of the girls who wore her tie with the biggest knot possible and staggered around on the highest platform-soled shoes. My work began to suffer and at the end of the first year my friends and I found ourselves in a lower class. It was awful, full of kids with no hope of achieving anything worthwhile. They verbally abused the teachers and had no interest in any of the lessons. I suddenly realized that if I was not careful I would end up like them. It was not a pleasant thought. I knew I had to do better and began to work hard. There were only about five out of a class of thirty who ever bothered to work and the rest of the class gave us all a bad time. However, the hard work was worth it as at the end of the second year I was reinstated in the higher class.

I began to take an interest in sport and to everyone's surprise became a very good cross-country runner. I had a place in the school team and started to win races. I found that I loved the game of hockey too. I played in goal, mainly because none of the other girls could be bothered to put on the pads and kickers needed in this position. When playing on the school team I soon discovered that not everyone played fairly and I often left the pitch at the end of a match bruised and bloodied.

By the time that I reached the fourth year at school I had to choose which subjects I would take at GCE O level. I knew that I did not want to go to university, but, like many of my friends, I did not have a clear idea of what I did want to do with my life. In the end I just chose the subjects that I really enjoyed – history, geography, art and biology and, of course like everyone else, I had to take maths and English.

Every month we had a careers lesson. Representatives from local companies would come to the school to tell us how good it would be to work for them. My friends began to talk about becoming clerks but the thought of being stuck in an office filled me with horror. I wanted to do something different but nothing interested me until the day that we had a visit from a female sergeant at the local Army recruiting office. She talked to us about joining the army and played a video that promoted the Women's Royal Army Corps. The minute I saw that video I was hooked. It showed a group of young women enjoying army life in an exotic location. They were obviously having fun lying on a beach and riding around on mopeds. Then there were a few shots of them in uniform. They looked so smart and the video implied that they were all earning a good wage and were living a carefree life in foreign parts. I decided right then that I wanted to take the Queen's shilling.

For weeks after I saw the video I kept pestering Mum about joining the army. Eventually in desperation she took me down to the careers office in the hope of dampening my enthusiasm. The sergeant was very nice to me but explained that, at only fifteen years old, I was too young to join. However, she did give me a lot of brochures to study. In those days women could not join individual regiments the way they can today. The only way to join was to apply to the WRAC. There were a number of different trades to follow within the WRAC but no matter which trade she chose each woman still wore the Lioness cap badge. I discovered that if I were to be accepted I could become anything from a hairdresser to a military policewoman. The list of opportunities seemed endless.

Much to Mum's amazement my enthusiasm for the army continued into my fifth year at school. At the end of that time I had managed to pass three O levels and three CSEs but I was still too young to join up. I resigned myself to another year at school and, hopefully, some more examination passes at the end of it. In reality I did very little, but I managed to pass three more O levels before saying goodbye to school for ever. I was delighted to be giving up rules, studying and uniforms at last. I went back to the army careers office where I was given a written test that I passed. I was then told that I would be asked to attend an assessment day in Guildford, Surrey.

The day soon arrived and, clutching my travel warrant, I set off on the first stage of my journey. Mum was convinced that I would get lost on the London underground but I managed the journey without mishap and eventually arrived in Guildford. Outside the station I found a group of girls who all looked as lost as I felt. A minibus soon arrived to take us to Queen Elizabeth Barracks, home of the WRAC.

We arrived to see a group of young women being drilled on the parade ground. They looked very smart in their immaculately pressed white shirts and green skirts. We spent the morning taking tests. I was a bit upset as I thought that there would be no more tests once I had left school. It did not take long for me to realize how naïve I had been. We spent a nervous lunchtime sitting in the cookhouse, each wondering how well she had done. The wait was not a long one. My name was called out and I went into a room with a small group of women. In front of the room stood a tall, slim Captain, her hair tied neatly in a bun. When she spoke they were the words that I had waited so long to hear,

'Well done, ladies. You have all passed the tests and will be offered career advice very shortly. The ladies outside will unfortunately not be staying with us.'

I was elated. I had made it at my first attempt and when it was my turn to discuss my career options I was still in a daze. The Military Police looked interesting to me but I was told immediately that, at five feet three inches tall, I was too short to be considered. The Captain told me that I had scored well in the tests and advised me to choose a career that would allow me to use my brain. She began to steer me towards the Royal Signals and I was eventually offered a position as a Data Telegraphist within the Signals. The Captain told me that it would involve five months' training but that the postings for such a trade were world-wide and that I would soon be sent abroad.

I was overjoyed and could hardy wait to get home to tell Mum. She, of course, was her usual down-to-earth self. She pointed out that there would be no one in the army to pick up my clothes or tidy my room. I would not listen to her. I was seventeen years old and quite grown up; I knew better than anyone else. I was in for the biggest shock of my life.

CHAPTER TWO

I left home on a Monday morning. It was a little like my first day at school although I was much too excited to be upset at the prospect of leaving home. Mum, on the other hand, was in tears, just as she had been years before when she had left me at the school gates. This time I was the one who was leaving, with all my belongings packed into two suitcases.

The shock of army life began for me the moment I walked through the gates of Queen Elizabeth barracks. I was bellowed at and marched, at the double, to the reception area. Suddenly the reality of my situation began to hit me. I was now Private George, the lowest of the low.

There were about ninety of us starting basic training, divided into three platoons. I was put into 7 Platoon with thirty other women. We shared accommodation, four to a room with communal showers and toilets.

Joining the army had been my dream for so long but suddenly I wanted to go home. I was desperately homesick and, for the first week at least, I could not telephone home. Even attempting to dial the number would leave me in floods of tears. Each night I wept into my pillow, bitterly regretting having left my comfortable home and my mother's loving care.

I had never before come across such a wide range of women. Most of them were two or three years older than I, with some work experience behind them. They talked a lot about the boyfriends they had left behind. I had never had a serious relationship before and was still a virgin. My experience was limited to the occasional snog or a quick grope. I kept very quiet while they discussed their boyfriends and prayed to God that no one would ask me to divulge any of my secrets.

There was a group of four or five girls who were very loud and soon began to rule the roost. When they spoke, their sentences were punctuated with obscenities, some of which I had never heard before. They picked a girl with whom I shared and began to bully her. No one knew what she had done to upset them. Perhaps they chose her because their victim had to be weaker than they were for the bullying to succeed.

For six weeks she endured their bullying and, in spite of having her belongings stolen and being thrown into a bath of cold water, she would not give in to them. I despised myself for letting them do it but could not think of a single thing that I could do to stop it and so remained silent, as did the rest of the platoon. Although the corporals and sergeants knew what was happening no one intervened on her behalf and the bullies were allowed to make her life miserable. I was terrified of them. I had come across bullies at school but this was something quite different.

The first week of training was spent getting our uniforms together. There was so much of it: summer shirts, winter shirts, shoes, best uniform, two hats, jumpers and coats. Everything had to be kept in an immaculate condition. I regretted that I had not been interested when Mum tried to show me how to iron collars and cuffs. Everything had to be ironed. Even our top blankets had to have a crease straight down the middle. Try as I might, my creases always looked like Blackpool tramlines. At eight o'clock each morning we were inspected by the officer in charge and by the sergeant. They found fault with everything. Even our wardrobes and drawers had to be laid out in a certain way which was difficult since we had all that uniform and only one wardrobe and four drawers each. Everything that we had brought with us had to be packed away in cases.

I had never hand-washed clothes before but I soon learned how to do it. Every night we each had to wash the shirt we had worn that day and our PT kit. There were no washing machines. We had four sinks and very limited drying space for the use of thirty women. Soon my fingers were red raw and smelled of the green carbolic soap that we had to use. Once our clothes had been washed, we turned our attention to the accommodation. Wooden floors were polished by hand and baths and showers had to be scrubbed. Everything smelled of polish and starch. As a group we quickly learned to pull together. No one wanted to be the one responsible for the others being confined to barracks. When I overcame my homesickness enough to telephone home I moaned constantly. Mum always listened patiently and never once said, 'I told you so!'

After a while I began to enjoy myself. We used to drill twice a day and there was also a lot of PT. I soon became very good at it and was allowed extra time at night to train. Army life was not all marching and cleaning. We were given basic training in map reading and using a compass. Then we were taken to a training area and each of us in turn had to take a map and a compass and march on a given bearing. None of us took it too seriously and we treated it as a day off.

We were given lessons in military history and were told how the modern army worked. At that time there was a lot of talk about the threat from Russia and so we practised nuclear, biological and chemical drills, NBC for short. It was a very grand title but all it really meant was that we had to put on combat gear and gas masks in the shortest time possible. It never seemed to occur to anyone that in a nuclear attack we would all be blown to smithereens anyway. All that mattered was that we managed to put on our gas masks in less than ten seconds.

One afternoon we attended a lecture on weapon training, given by a sergeant from the Guards depot. He was a huge man, six feet tall and seemingly just as wide. He showed us the standard weapons used by the army at that time: the sub-machine gun, the self-loading rifle and the 9mm pistol. He told us not to worry about any other weapons as only men were allowed to use them. When he left we asked our sergeant why women were not allowed to carry guns. She explained that women were used only in support roles and were non-combatant. This was a big disappointment to me as I began to realize that I would never be in the thick of the action and that the closest I would come to anything exciting would be the yearly exercises.

During that first six weeks I even managed to master the art of ironing and shoe polishing and soon the first part of our training was over. On pass out day Mum, Hazel, Bob and Grandma all came down to watch the parade. It was a glorious September day and I felt so proud as I marched past my family. By late afternoon the visitors had all left and I felt a huge sense of anticlimax as we sat about and wondered what the next phase of our training would be like.

This was the last time that we would all be together and there were many tears shed that afternoon. I was sent to Catterick with Sarah, one of the other girls from 7 Platoon. The day after the parade we set off for Catterick garrison with six girls from the other two platoons. I was amazed by the size of Catterick. The camp seemed endless with a huge variety of regiments stationed there. My home for the next five months was 8 Signal Regiment at Vimy Barracks and it was the biggest camp I had ever seen. Queen Elizabeth Barracks, by comparison, was very small and modern and, of course, there had been no men. 8 Signals was housed in three-storey blocks surrounded by moorland. The women's accommodation was a two-storey, red-brick building in the centre of the camp. It was called Katherine House but was known to all as 'The Kennel'.

The next phase of my training began and I soon discovered what life as a Data Telegraphist was like. I worked in a communications centre, or commcen for short. I was responsible for receiving messages in a written form. I then had to type them in a signal format. As I typed a perforated paper tape was produced and it was this tape that was sent through relays for onward transmission. Incoming messages were handled in the same way with a hard copy and a tape for back-up. Although it sounded quite simple, I soon discovered that there was a lot of technical data that had to be learned. Data telegraphists also had to know how to operate a switchboard and, at that time, the Army was still using an old-fashioned pull cord system.

Most of the signal-based trades were taught at 8 Signals. The data telegraphists' training took longer than most and so we considered that the other trades like radio operators were beneath us and treated them as such. In the NAAFI we sat in a group by ourselves and ignored everyone else. The only time that we mixed with the others was on disco nights.

Because very few of us had cars and the nearest towns, Richmond and Darlington, could only be reached by long bus rides, we were virtually confined to camp. All the nearest pubs were out of bounds and so our social lives revolved around the NAAFI. We had film nights, but the most popular entertainment was the discos. They gave us the chance to get dressed up and have a few 'lager and blacks'.

I met my first serious boyfriend while I was at Catterick. He was a Brian Ferry fan and wore the same slicked back hairstyle and shiny suits, with the sleeves pushed up. We used to dance to all the slow numbers or sometimes just sit and hold hands. Then he would walk me back to 'the Kennel' where we would find a spot against the wall, between the other couples. I had to be in by ten thirty so we would just have time for a quick snog before the doors were locked.

Every evening we women were bed-checked. If we were not in by the time the doors were locked we would be on a charge the next day. This rule did not apply to the men, who could do what they liked. I was still under eighteen and, although I did not like the rule, I could see why it might apply to minors. However, some of my friends were in their twenties and were still treated like children.

One night one of my roommates, Wendy, did not come in on time. My best friend, Des, and I sat up to wait for her. Sarah, as usual, was fast asleep. The duty corporal came in and wanted to know where Wendy was. We could only say that we did not know. The next morning she was still missing. We went to our lessons and found that the course sergeant was also missing. It was not long before we discovered that they had been having an affair and had become engaged. In spite of their plans to marry, the official Army rule was that they could not have a relationship and so Wendy, who was twenty-five years old, was forced to resign.

This was just another example of the double standards that were applied to men and women. We were all delighted when we heard that, in spite of their difficulties, they had got married.

The rest of the course passed without incident and we were soon looking forward to our first posting. The course before us had all been sent overseas so hopes were high. When the posting came through I was told that I was too young to be sent abroad and was posted to a small signal squadron a few miles down the road in York. Kath, Chris and Tanya joined me there but my best friend, Des, was sent to Cyprus. All the others went to Germany.

CHAPTER THREE

I was really disappointed not to be going abroad, but, as I was discovering more and more, it was a case of 'put up and shut up'.

The signal squadron to which we were posted was based at Imphal Barracks in York. The squadron itself was very small, only ten DTGs and four switchboard operators. We were put in the charge of a lance corporal and two male corporals who were married and lived off camp. We saw very little of the men. A major and a captain who looked after the day-to-day events ran the squadron.

Our living quarters were terrible and we had to share, six to a room. The ceilings were very high and there were strip lights that buzzed incessantly. I hated it there. We moved our sparse furniture to try to create some private areas but it proved impossible.

Every Monday night was 'bull' night when we had to clean our rooms and the rest of the block. This was a ritual that I had had to perform every week since I had joined the army and I began to hate it. At eight o'clock the duty sergeant would come round to inspect the rooms. If she was in a good mood we would be allowed to go to the NAAFI but if not we would be stuck in the block for the rest of the night. Some of the sergeants took great pleasure in finding faults. They would wear white gloves and wipe their hands over surfaces looking for dust; some would tilt mirrors, searching for the smallest smear. The next morning we would have to go through the same charade with a rookie lieutenant.

For me it was worse than for most of the girls as I was still under eighteen and had to undergo a bed check at ten thirty each night. If I wanted to go into town with the others I had to beg the

Sergeant for a special pass until midnight. This was a humiliation reserved for females alone. The men never suffered this indignity and even had civilians to clean their block for them.

There was an even more sinister side to the Army that I discovered very early one morning. We were woken by shouts and by the lights being turned on. The room was filled with Military Police who flung open wardrobe doors and pulled blankets off the beds. I was ordered out of bed and told to open up my wardrobe. An MP began searching through my belongings, examining all my clothes and letters very carefully. I had no idea what they expected to find. Eventually the MP seemed to be satisfied that I had nothing of interest and so moved on to the next bed. Just then our Sergeant arrived and told us that it was an SIB raid and that we should co-operate fully. Over fifty women were made to get out of bed and each room was searched.

The next day the talk was of nothing else and we then heard that two corporals had been taken away. I naively asked why and was told by one of the drivers that it was 'because they were dykes'. I began to think that I must have been going around with my eyes shut because I had never seen the slightest indication that there were any lesbians in the barracks. It had not occurred to me that there might be and I could not see why it would matter anyway. The two corporals were dismissed just because they were gay and no one seemed to care that they were good at their jobs.

There were a number of one-man commcens scattered throughout our region that were manned by civilians. One of our duties was to provide cover when one of the civilian staff went on holiday. Because we were new to the job we first had to gain some experience at the York commcen. This was a major, 24-hour communications centre, staffed by shifts of civilians. Despite the fact that most of them were ex-Army, they loathed us. Because of our inexperience we had to be accompanied at all times and these babysitting duties just made their busy lives even more hectic.

We all managed to get through the first month without any major mishaps and it was decided that we were ready to be sent out on our own. We were away for between one week and one month and often the commcens were located in barracks without any female accommodation, which meant that we had to live in digs outside the camp. Occasionally we were allowed to stay in the Sergeants' Mess provided we remembered our places. It was a lonely existence, shut up in a secure room all day. Our only contact with the outside world at these times was when the dispatch clerk came to collect or deliver the signals. I became very despondent and disillusioned with life in the army. This was not why I had joined and I wanted to do something a bit more exciting.

Then, in April, 1982, Argentinian forces invaded the Falkland Islands and the single company of Royal Marines that was guarding the capital, Port Stanley, was overwhelmed. Suddenly our armed forces were mobilized and went off to the South Atlantic to fight. I was sure that this would be my opportunity for a posting that would allow me to see some action at last. I was right in one sense, for I was posted. When the Engineer Regiment shipped out of Ripon, I moved in to man another commcen. Once again I was stuck in the barracks, becoming more and more frustrated.

As a mere private I was considered to be the lowest of the low. Above me, but only slightly more important, were the lance corporals and corporals. Next came the sergeants and warrant officers who had their own facilities, quite separate from ours. Then there were officers whose lives and careers were completely different from all the rest. They each had their own room with a civilian cleaner. Waiters or waitresses served their meals and most had their washing and ironing done for them. There was no such thing as a bed check or a bull night for an officer; they lived in a different world. These were the people in charge of us and, for most of the time, they treated us like idiots.

Many of the officers came from upper class backgrounds and spoke with refined accents. For this reason we referred to them as 'Rupert' or 'Rodney'. A lot were arrogant, self-important fools who had joined the army on three-year short-term commissions before returning to civilian life to work in the family business. Their private education and privileged backgrounds did not enable them to be good leaders, but, for some reason, these were the types of people that the Army liked to recruit as officers. Some had such superior attitudes that they refused to speak to the lowest ranks and would only communicate through a sergeant or corporal. A few did speak directly, but usually raised their voices slightly and spoke in short, simple sentences as if they were dealing with people with learning disabilities.

Problems often arose when young officers, straight out of training, were put in charge of seasoned troops. It was quite normal for them to give orders that would be received with a smile and a salute and then carried out in a completely different way to that envisaged by the officer. Needless to say, there was a lot of animosity between the non-commissioned ranks and the officers.

While I was stationed at Fulford Barracks in York an officer, completely unlike the rest, was put in charge of the women. Captain T was like a breath of fresh air. She was in her late twenties, slim, sporty and full of new ideas. She spoke to us without a trace of condescension and managed to motivate us all.

I had become heavily involved in sport and was already the North-east area cross-country champion. Captain T encouraged me to train for the Army Championships. Although she had asthma herself, she would often come out training with me in the evenings. As I became more and more involved in sport I began to think about becoming a PTI. Captain T, however, had other plans for me.

One day, in the summer of 1982, we were having lunch in the cookhouse when a group of six women dressed in full combat gear came in. We usually dressed in shirts, skirts and berets and left our combat gear for the yearly exercises, so the sight of these women caused a lot of curiosity. Since officers never came into our cookhouse, we were even more surprised to see Captain T follow them in. They did not mix with anyone outside their own group and, after a hurried meal, left again as mysteriously as they had arrived. We discovered that they were all sharing a room and, although they remained in the barracks for the rest of the week, they never spoke to anyone outside their own group at all.

A week or so later I was summoned to Captain T's office. I was always apprehensive about calls such as this and immediately thought that I must have done something wrong. Captain T was busily writing as I walked in and saluted her and, without looking up, she told me to sit. I waited until she finished her writing and I must have looked nervous because she immediately said, 'Don't look so worried. I want to talk to you about your career.' I began to relax until she continued, 'I don't think that being a PTI would be the best move for you.'

Suddenly I felt so depressed. Sport had become the most important thing to me and I was sick of my work as a DTG. Captain T, however, had not finished. She handed me a piece of paper, headed PROJECT ALPHA with the words, 'I think you ought to consider another option.'

I quickly read that volunteers were needed for special duties in Northern Ireland and asked Captain T what exactly 'special duties' meant. She told me that the six women I had seen the previous week were volunteers and that, if they completed their course successfully, they would be sent to Northern Ireland to work in a covert role. She was not able to tell me any more but added that she thought it was something that I could do and advised me to go away and think about it. She told me to let her know of my decision as soon as possible.

When the weekly orders were published a few days later, I noticed that tucked away at the end was a paragraph asking for volunteers for Project Alpha, with all reports to be sent to Captain T. I did not want to appear to be too interested in front of the other women but when I read out the orders and no one reacted to the paragraph I had to ask if anyone knew what it meant. They all shrugged their shoulders. I decided to volunteer and put my report in to Captain T. Whilst out training that evening, she came over to me and told me that she thought I had made the right choice.

Quite unexpectedly I was told that I was being sent on the next available driving course at the Army School of Driving in Leconfield. This caused quite a stir amongst the other girls. I had never shown any interest in driving but some of the others had applied for the course and now I was the one to be given a place. They could not understand why I was going when they had been turned down. I tried to appear innocent and just shrugged my shoulders.

Leconfield was an ex RAF base and it was here that most of the driver training for the Army took place. The closest I had ever come to driving a car was when, as a child, I used to sit next to Bob in his Cortina and play with a toy steering wheel.

All the driving instructors were civilians and I was lucky enough to be taught by one who was extremely patient. I spent the first day lurching around the runways in a Chevette trying to master the clutch.

The next two weeks were spent out on the roads, driving for miles every day. I began to enjoy myself, in spite of having to wear my uniform. It was summertime and the weather was hot, too hot to wear a beret. However, it was part of my uniform and I was not allowed to remove it. Nor was I allowed to take my hands from the steering wheel and so had to cope with sweat trickling into my eyes from underneath my beret. I coped and soon felt confident enough to take my test.

The day of the test arrived and, almost immediately, the nightmare began. I made one small mistake and started to panic. Then everything began to go wrong. When it came to the hill start I revved the engine, released the handbrake and rolled back down the hill. I knew I had failed but when the examiner confirmed my worst fears I burst into tears. This was my first failure and I knew that my chance of a new career was rapidly diminishing.

I was despondent as I returned to the block to pack my belongings before returning to York. Then I was summoned to the Chief Instructor's office. The sergeant shook his head, called me a twat and then told me to be ready to re-take the test the following day. I could hardly believe my luck. The sergeant's parting words were, 'Somebody likes you, George. Now, fuck off!'

The next day I passed my test, much to the delight of my instructor. He was waiting for me on my return with a large box of tissues, just in case!

When I returned to York, Sue, the Lance Corporal in charge

of the office, met me. She told me to collect my movement boxes and pack my kit as I was being posted and would be leaving in a week. She wanted to know what was going on. I was amazed that everything was happening so fast but could tell her nothing other than that I had volunteered for special duties. Sue helped me and between us we packed my kit into three large packing cases. My bed space was suddenly empty. I went over to see Captain T and she told me that once I started on the course I would probably never return to York and that packing my kit was a precaution against that eventuality.

The last few days passed by quickly and, although I was excited to be going, it was upsetting to be leaving my friends behind. My last weekend was spent trying to have a drink in every one of the 365 pubs in York.

CHAPTER FOUR

I arrived early on a Monday morning and, after my hectic weekend, I had a thumping headache.

I was one of six women to arrive that day and we were driven in a minibus to the camp. No one was in uniform, but, from the way everyone was dressed, I could tell that there was only one officer among the six. She was the tall, thin one with glasses who was wearing a skirt and blouse. No one but an officer would dress like that. The rest of us were in standard 'squaddie' gear, jeans and sweatshirts.

The drive to camp was short and when we arrived we were taken directly to a set of portakabins behind the Sergeants' Mess. We were not even required to stop at the guardhouse to book in. Instead we hauled our luggage into the portakabin in which we were to live for the next week, sharing four to a room. We had no time to look around before we were called to attend a briefing.

Two men walked into the briefing room, both dressed as civilians. The taller of the two introduced himself as Bob. The smaller, dark man was called Jason. We were told that we were to call them 'Staff' at all times and that we should address each other by our first names. We were also instructed not to talk to each other about our backgrounds, our work or anything else that would lead to us being identified. Bob and Jason stressed that they would know if these rules had been disobeyed and that the culprit would be returned to unit immediately.

At the end of the briefing we were told to change into PT kit for a basic fitness test. This was a run of one and a half miles that had to be completed in thirteen and a half minutes. We all passed that first test without any problems. When we got back to our portakabin, Bob told us to remove any form of identification from our combat gear. Even our ranks had to remain a secret. The first evening spent in each others company was quite strained. Since we were not allowed to talk about anything that would give any hint of our identities, no one knew what to say.

The next day we went to a classroom where Bob told us that we were to be given a map-reading test. We were each given a 1:25,000 scale map, a set of coloured pencils and a test paper. I was quite happy. While I had been at York I had practised my map-reading skills and was quite confident that I would pass this test with flying colours.

I looked at the first question and thought how easy it was, 'What colour is a main trunk road? Draw your answer.'

I drew a red line and went on to the next question and then the one after that. They were all easy. I completed all ten questions and handed my test paper to Bob, smugly thinking how well I had done.

Bob collected all of the test papers and went through them. When he finally spoke I was shocked by his words. 'Crap', he said. 'None of you has got more than half the questions right. Are you surprised? You should be.' He continued, 'An A road may be shown in red but there is a faint black border to it which you have all missed. Ladies, you will learn that attention to detail is paramount.'

We spent the rest of the day learning how to use a Silva compass and working out bearings.

The following day we were given the chance to practice our new skills at a local training area. That evening we began to learn about navigating in vehicles in the dark. Bob took three of us and the other three, of whom I was one, went with Jason. We drove off into the countryside. It was pitch black outside the car when Jason pulled over into a lay-by and explained what he wanted us to do. We took turns to navigate. Jason showed us on the map where we were at that moment. He then showed us where he wanted to get to and we were given sixty seconds to select a route and to memorize it. The two points were five or six miles apart and there were numerous roads and lanes in between.

When it was my turn, my mind went numb but I tried hard to concentrate. Jason unfolded the map and showed me where he wanted to go. I began to work out a route: third left, first right, straight on. After what seemed like only a few seconds, Jason suddenly said, 'Time's up. Let's go.'

I knew that I was not ready but started to give him directions anyway. Almost immediately we turned into a country lane with high banks and hedges. I found it hard to remember which route I had intended to take. It was completely dark except for our headlights and everything looked different from what I had expected it to be. Jason pulled over and asked me if I knew where I was. I looked at the map but I really had no idea and shrugged my shoulders in embarrassment. He had known all the time that I was lost but told me not to worry, as I would be getting lots of practice and would soon be able to find my way around.

The fourth day was devoted to an intensive weapon-training session on the range. The standard weapons of the day, the SLR, the SMG and the 9mm pistol, were laid out in front of us. Bob and Jason showed us how to strip and reassemble each weapon and placed great emphasis on safety. We went through this drill many times before we were even shown the ammunition. Once that had been introduced they made sure that we checked each weapon, removing live rounds and magazines whenever the gun was picked up. Then it was time for us to fire the weapons. I found to my surprise that I was quite a good shot.

The remainder of the week flew by and on Friday afternoon I was fairly confident about my night navigation and weapon-handling ability. Bob told us that we were free to return home for the weekend and advised us to go straight home and not return to our units. He also cautioned us against speaking to anyone about the past week. He then wished us luck and told us to report at 10am on the following Monday morning to Camp Alpha. I collected my travel warrant from the chief clerk and made my way home.

Mum was delighted to see me and, as usual, her first questions were, 'How long have you got?' and 'Where is your washing?'

Without thinking I began to tell Mum what I had been doing. I told her about volunteering for special duties and went on to say that if I were successful I would soon be off to Northern Ireland. Mum's face fell and she became very quiet. Too late I realized how insensitive I had been. At that time Northern Ireland was always in the news. Hardly a day passed without some report of bombings and the murders of policemen or soldiers. No wonder that Mum was worried. I could see the thoughts going through her head as she imagined my body being returned to her in a flag-draped coffin. We spent an uneasy weekend. Mum could not understand why I had volunteered. She would have been happy for me to go to Germany or to Cyprus, but why Northern Ireland? I found it hard to explain to her. I just knew that it was something I had to do.

The following Monday, a dull, misty October day, I reported to Camp Alpha. I was shown to the reception area. The desk clerk checked a list of names and informed me that I was no longer Private George but would, henceforth, be known as 190. I must have looked puzzled as he handed me a plastic-coated badge with the number 190 on it and said, 'That's right. You are a number now. Here's your badge, so you won't forget.' He pushed a form towards me and told me to sign it. 'It's a disclaimer,' he explained. 'If you fuck up or get hurt, you've got no comeback. Don't forget, you are a volunteer.'

Alarm bells began to ring in my head. This did not make sense nor was it fair. Why should I sign away my rights to anything, just because I had volunteered? However, I realized that the clerk had been giving an order not a request and so I signed the form anyway and was ushered into another room. Behind a desk sat two WRAC sergeants. 'Number?' one of them barked. '190, Sergeant,' I replied. 'Well, 190, when you get to your accommodation you will make sure that everything that identifies you and everything of a personal nature is put into this envelope and handed to me. Is that clear?' I answered that it was and, as I left the room, I could hear the other sergeant say in a stage whisper, 'She's no fucking chance!'

I was glad to be outside again and looked around at what would be my home for the next two weeks. It was a dump; row upon row of wooden huts and the perimeter fence topped with barbed wire. It looked like a POW camp from an old war film. I made my way to the female quarters and was pleased to see that one of the other girls, Leanne, had already arrived. She and I had become quite friendly in the short time we had been together. She was tall with short blonde hair and a dry sense of humour. She beckoned to me from the far end of the room and pointed out the cobwebs hanging from the ceiling and the filthy window. We unpacked quickly and put all our personal items into envelopes as we had been instructed. Then we changed into our combat gear and sat on our beds waiting for our next instructions.

At exactly 10am the door burst open and the two women sergeants walked in. We leapt up and stood to attention. They began their inspection. Lucy, another colleague from the previous week, was the first to incur their wrath. The smaller of the sergeants began rummaging through Lucy's case. She pulled out a paperback book and flicked through the pages, stopping at an inscription inside the cover. 'Isn't this nice?' she said, 'To Lucy, with lots of love.' In an instant her expression changed. She ripped off the cover and thrust it into Lucy's face. 'Fucking imbecile,' she screamed. 'Can't you understand orders? I know who you are now, don't I? Get down and give me twenty press-ups!'

One by one, all our belongings were searched and the sergeants recovered all sorts of things that we had overlooked. Then it was my turn. I was beginning to think I had got away with it when suddenly a bus ticket was pulled from the pocket at the side of my holdall. The small sergeant turned to me, a sarcastic smile on her face, 'Now I know where you come from, dickhead. Give me twenty press-ups, go!' For a small woman she had a very powerful voice that she used again as she walked towards the door. 'Get your arses outside, NOW!'

We doubled outside and I was amazed to see at least two hundred men lining up and marking time. A voice gave the order to stop and through the mist a major, flanked by at least twenty sergeants, came into view. He introduced himself as the Training

Major and told us that the sergeants were to be referred to as DS (Directing Staff) at all times. I looked across at the DS and could see that they came from a number of different regiments. There were the maroon berets of the Parachute Regiment, the green of the Marines and the brown of the Guards. Some I could not recognize and one, I later discovered, was from the Royal Navy.

The Major began to speak. 'Ladies and gentlemen,' he said. 'I will remind you that you are all volunteers. The next two weeks are not for the faint-hearted. I personally don't care who you are or where you come from. That doesn't matter. You are all equal. Just numbers. You can leave at any time and, believe me, most of you will, one way or another.' He turned to a tall, athletically built PTI from the Parachute Regiment and concluded, 'Now, Staff. Explain to these people exactly what is expected.'

The Para stepped forward and I was immediately struck by his resemblance to Bruce Forsyth. He looked down his nose at the assembled ranks and began to explain the rules and regulations. There was to be no fraternization and no contact with the outside world. All incoming and outgoing mail would be vetted. There was no time off, no alcohol, lights were turned out at 11pm and so it went on. I began to wonder what I had let myself in for. Nothing I had experienced in my previous army life had prepared me for this.

The DS finished his lecture and we were called out by number to form squads. I was with about thirty men and one other woman, Liz. We doubled away, the DS harassing us like wolves around frightened sheep.

Running in squad is always difficult, as you have to judge the length of your stride so as not to clip the heels of the person in front. I was in the middle of the squad and the youth behind kept clipping my boot and causing me to stumble. When the DS saw what was happening he halted the squad and parted the rank in front of me. 'You spastic', he screamed, spittle flying in all directions. I was so shocked at his outburst that I made the mistake of looking directly at him. He exploded again, 'Don't look at me, girly. Get down and give me twenty.' I dropped to the floor and began pushing up. The DS looked around and began bellowing,

'So you think it's funny, do you, fuck-face? All of you get down!' All around me bodies began dropping to the floor. The DS was screaming like someone demented. I had never before heard such hatred in a voice and it shocked me.

When all the press-ups were complete we started to run again. We ran for a mile or two and then finished with more press-ups and sit-ups. During the entire time the DS was shouting abuse at us. I was drenched with sweat, mostly from fear I think. When we got back to the assembly area we were ordered to put on PT kit and be back within five minutes.

We rushed inside, frantically pulling off our sweaty clothes and diving into PT kit. I dreaded being the last one to return but need not have worried. I was relieved to find there were quite a few still missing. The last to get back was a young man who was made to run up and down our ranks, shouting 'I'm a wanker' at the top of his voice.

We stood shivering for a long while, waiting for all the other squads to return. They were then subjected to the same abuse that we had suffered. At last everyone was assembled. By now the mist had turned to steady drizzle and we were all cold and wet. The Training Major returned and, with a smile, yelled,

'Combats. Five minutes. Into the cookhouse. GO.' In the frenzy of activity I heard Leanne muttering, 'I wish they would make up their bleedin' minds.'

I exchanged one set of wet clothes for another and ran over to the cookhouse. It occupied a huge area and doubled as a gym. Naturally we all tried to sit together for mutual comfort but the DS soon realized what was happening and made us split up, informing us that we were not in a ladies' knitting circle. Each table contained pens and piles of paper. We sat around in our steaming, damp clothes waiting to be told what was expected of us next.

Before long a tall, skinny DS wearing glasses and the plumed beret of the Fusiliers explained. 'Essay time for those of you that can read and write. Those who can't had better fuck off now.' He paused and looked around, obviously expecting some of us to leave. When no one moved he looked disappointed and continued, 'Write down exactly what you think special duties is all about. You have half an hour.'

I thought about what I would write and the best that I could manage was to say that I would be working in a covert role against the IRA. Somehow I managed to fill one and a half sheets of A4 paper on the subject. I noticed that some of the others had written much less than me. One of the lads on my table had only written a few lines and, when the DS collected the papers, he looked at this one, shook his head and murmured, 'Thick bastard'.

The rest of the day was taken up with fitness and other gym tests. By five o'clock that afternoon at least ten of the men had packed their bags and left. We women spent a relatively quiet evening trying to clean up our hut. Leanne and I were looking around for some bedding when Liz suddenly said, 'Don't bother making the beds. Just put down your maggots (sleeping bags). Trust me.'

We pounced on her, wanting to know what she meant, but she would say no more. Lucy accused her of being a mole but she just laughed. When we eventually turned in we noticed that Liz just removed her boots but kept on her damp combats. We thought it best to follow her lead and so settled down for the night.

I soon forgot how uncomfortable it was to wear damp clothes and fell into a deep sleep. Suddenly I felt someone shake me and awoke to see the blonde Sergeant, finger to her lips, silently indicating that I was not to make a sound. I sat up and she beckoned to me. As my eyes became accustomed to the dark I was surprised to see some of my roommates on the floor doing press-ups. I joined them and watched as, one by one, the others were awakened. When everyone was wide awake the lights were put on and the Sergeant shouted, 'MOVE . . . Outside now!'

I found my boots and slipped them on but did not have time to tie the laces before running outside to begin marking time. Arc lights illuminated the camp and from every hut the men poured out, accompanied by the screaming obscenities of the DS. When we were all assembled, we were marched off to another building.

We filed in to a room in semi-darkness. Ahead of me I could see row upon row of wooden chairs and, at the front of the room, a large white screen. From the back came the voice of the DS telling us that we were going to see a film. Instinctively I looked at my wrist. Of course, my watch was not there. It was in an envelope, locked away somewhere along with all my other possessions and those of my companions. Later I learned that this was a sensory deprivation technique, designed to break the more weak-willed among us.

The lights were extinguished and the film began. It was a black and white documentary and looked as if it dated back to the 1930s. A colonial couple were expounding the virtues of bamboo and listing its numerous uses. Around me heads began to drop and I could hear the sound of gentle snoring. I managed to stay awake and was glad that I had when, after twenty minutes, the film ended and the DS told us we would have to answer some questions about it. He handed out papers and pens and began to reel off twenty questions. I managed to answer most of them. The test papers were collected and we had to wait while they were marked. By now I was so tired I was almost numb.

When the marking was complete, the DS called out the numbers of those of us who had scored ten or more. I was relieved to hear my number called and felt sorry for those who had obviously failed. They were subjected to yet more abuse from the DS. Back in the hut none of us found it easy to get back to sleep and we lay on our beds in silence, waiting for the night to pass.

CHAPTER FIVE

The next morning we were called at seven o'clock and made our way over to the cookhouse for breakfast. The food looked quite good and I decided to have scrambled eggs on toast and a large mug of tea. I did not want to make the mistake of having a big breakfast only to find that they intended to 'beast' (exercise) us directly afterwards. We ate and then sat around wondering what would happen next. We had not been waiting for very long when a DS came in and shouted at us to get outside in full combats. We were again put into mixed squads.

I was curious about my companions and tried to guess who they were. Most appeared to be NCOs. The telltale patch on their right arms where they had removed their stripes gave them away. One of the men was obviously an officer. His hair was slightly longer than that of the others and he wore a green cravat. He had an arrogant air and stood with his hands on his hips. As soon as I saw him I knew what would happen next. I was right. The DS came across and shouted at him, 'You – hands on hips! Get down.' The officer paused for a moment, trying to decide whether or not to say something. He left it a second too long and the DS, his face inches away from that of the officer, began to scream at him. 'Shithead! On the floor now or do I put you there? Oh, and by the way, Rupert. Get that fucking cravat off, you homo.' The lads grinned and I was surprised to see the DS smile and wink at us as the officer hit the floor.

This particular DS wore the beret of a Para and the tracksuit of a PTI. He was huge and had the flattest nose I had ever seen. His hair stood up in spiky tufts. He reminded me a lot of the comic character Dennis the Menace. As the officer lay panting on the floor the DS reached down and, with one hand, lifted him up by his collar. 'Twat!' he screeched, 'what are you?' The officer replied miserably, 'A twat, Staff.'

The DS turned to the rest of the group and told us that we would all be required to complete a number of tasks that day. We would each be given, in turn, overall responsibility for a set task and would be assessed on how well we performed. Although we were allowed to accept help this would count against us when it came to our assessments.

Once again the weather had not been kind to us. It was raining and before long we were all soaked.

Our first task seemed relatively simple. We were given a piece of rope, some planks of wood and three scaffold poles and were told that we had to take a wounded man over an imaginary ravine using only that equipment. It did not take long to accomplish the task and we set off again, stopping when we came to a river bank. There were three Directing Staff waiting for us, one of whom was Dennis the Menace. He, like the others, was smirking as he explained that our next task was to cross the river with an injured man and to keep all of our kit dry. We were given some oil drums to make a raft for the crossing and some bin liners to keep our kit dry.

I suddenly realized that I would have to take off my clothes and my heart sank. The lads in my squad were already starting to take off their clothes. From behind me I heard the sound of the DS's voice mocking me, 'Come on girly,' he said. 'Get your kit off.'

I began to strip off, my face scarlet with embarrassment. The lads were already down to their underpants and were stuffing their kit into the bin liners. By the time that I had removed all of my outer clothing they were already beginning to construct the raft. I was cold and covered with goose pimples. From somewhere a voice said, '190, you look like a plucked chicken.' Behind me I could hear the sound of laughter.

Clad only in my bra and knickers, I stuffed the rest of my clothes into a bin liner and began to help the lads to lash the drums together. When it was finished we heaved the raft over the bank and slithered into the water after it. It was freezing and as we moved forward the water became deeper and deeper. I gritted my teeth and ducked under until it reached my shoulders. The cold took my breath away. Underfoot the riverbed was coated in slimy, oozing mud and every few steps we grazed our bare feet on sharp rocks.

Eventually we reached the far side of the river and clambered out, pulling our raft behind us. We stood in a small huddle, shivering and wondering what we were supposed to do next. Through the mist across the river came the voice of the DS yelling at us to come back. Our group leader groaned and, through gritted teeth, muttered, 'Bastards' before we plunged into the icy water once more.

We emerged on the other side, cold, wet and miserable, to find that there were no towels for us to dry ourselves. We patted ourselves down with our combat jackets but it made no difference because they were wet anyway. There is no worse feeling than that of damp clothes on a wet, dirty body. I had trouble getting my trousers on and my shirt began to chafe under my arms. As if that were not bad enough, the DS was already screaming at us to hurry up and we set off again for the next test.

At last it was my turn. I was given two planks of wood and a metal pole and was told that I had to retrieve an item stuck on another pole in the middle of a pond. This was a new situation for me and one I found rather daunting. I was surrounded by men who I knew to be superior to me in rank and I had to give them orders. I hesitated and, behind me, one of the men began to whisper instructions. I found it very difficult to give orders. It was much easier to ask them to do something than to tell them and, consequently, we ran out of time. The DS came over to me and instead of shouting, merely said, 'Don't be so fucking nice, 190.'

I went back to our hut and was surprised to find I was the first there. I took full advantage of the situation and stood under a hot shower, letting the warmth soothe my aching limbs. One by one the other girls returned, but not all of them had the luxury of a shower. The last one to get back just had time to tell us that we had to get into our combats and get straight outside again for the afternoon session.

We were organized into different mixed groups and set off along one of the many tracks around the camp. As I jogged I allowed my mind to wander. Suddenly, to my left, there was a loud bang. Some of the squad dived for cover; others stood frozen like rabbits caught in a car's headlights. I fell over the man in front of me who had flung himself to the ground when he heard the bang. From within a bush at the edge of the track a voice yelled, 'Get up', and was followed by the appearance of two Directing Staff. I was dismayed to see that one of them was the bespectacled one we had named Mr Sneer. The other was an evil looking Para with a thick, drooping moustache which gave him the appearance of a Mexican bandit.

Mr Sneer looked at us and announced, 'Most of you are now dead!' He then turned to his colleague and muttered, 'Pity it's not the real thing. We could have got rid of most of these wasters.' They both sniggered and then Mr Sneer said, 'The sound you have just heard was a flash bang. It sounds like a grenade but unless you stick it up your arse, it won't kill you.' He turned and we followed him on to a firing range where a number of self-loading rifles and sub-machine guns had been laid out. We were told to pick up a weapon and to make it safe. I was suddenly glad of the training I had already done as the drill was still fresh in my mind. I could remember exactly what I had to do.

Mr Sneer came along the line inspecting the SLRs that we were holding with the cocking lever back to show that the weapon was clear. He stopped in front of me and looked me up and down. A sneer spread across his face. 'God help us,' he said. 'A woman and a cripple!' I flushed scarlet. I was the only one in the squad who was left-handed and I was holding the rifle in the opposite hand to all the others. He shook his head and continued down the line until he reached Liz. He was obviously enjoying himself by now. 'Good God!' he bellowed, 'I hope you don't hold your boyfriend's cock like that. Grip it, woman!'

Time after time we went through the various weapon drills. When we stripped the guns down it was against the clock.

However well we performed this task it was always too slow for Mr Sneer. He abused us at every opportunity. I was beginning to lose my concentration and my fingers were cold. I fumbled and the working parts of the rifle shot forward, trapping my finger. I pulled my hand away but I was too late to stop the blood that poured from a deep cut in my finger. Before I had the chance to do anything about it the clock started again and Mr Sneer walked up and down the line shouting at us to hurry. He stopped in front of me again and looked at the blood running down my hand and on to the rifle. 'Like I said, 190, you're a cripple,' was his only comment.

The lesson finished with another comment from Mr Sneer about how slow we had been. Then we set off at the double for the cookhouse. We were covered in oil and mud, and by now my finger was throbbing. When we arrived we found that the taller of the two WRAC sergeants was waiting for us and we sat down with two other squads. She told us that we were to be tested on weapon recognition. She showed us twenty slides of various weapons and told us to write down what we thought they were. I recognized the Lee Enfield rifle and the German Luger pistol, used by every Nazi in all the war films I had seen. Unfortunately, I did not recognize any of the other eighteen slides. When the slide show finished we swapped papers and marked each other's. We all did very badly and the sergeant told us that none of us had recognized the weapons most commonly used by terrorists.

A table was brought into the room and on it were a number of different weapons. The sergeant picked up each of them in turn and showed us how they worked. I was amazed at her knowledge and the fact that she handled each of them in such a capable manner. It was an interesting lesson and I was sorry that it soon came to an end. From the back of the room I recognized the barking tones of the DS who looked like Bruce Forsyth and we all jumped to our feet. The next group was already coming into the room. I spotted Leanne, red-faced and sweating. She looked across at me and shook her head.

My group filed outside and was given five minutes to change into PT kit and get to the gym. I arrived to find that a huge circuit had been laid out and our circuit training began. There was no escape; the directing staff made sure that we all pushed ourselves as hard as we could. After forty-five minutes every muscle ached and I was breathing hard and dripping with sweat. I was not alone. The smell of hot, sweating bodies was overpowering. We had barely had the chance to recover from this exertion when the order was given for us to change into combat gear once more and be back within five minutes.

My legs felt like jelly as I ran to the hut to change my clothes. My combat gear was damp and smelly. I knew that I was beginning to smell like a polecat myself. We stood in line waiting for all the other squads to join us. When they were all assembled a DS began shouting out numbers. As each number was called that person fell out and marched away. Then the rest of us were dismissed.

Back in our hut we crowded around Liz and asked her if she knew what the next step would be. She told us that she had a friend who had gone through the course and that this was how she had known what would happen. She said that she did not really know any more but she was sure that, whatever it was, it would be awful.

Since we had not been told what to do we sat around in our hut, still wearing our filthy combat gear. Teatime came and we went over to the cookhouse, each of us aware of how bad we smelled. Mealtimes were usually noisy affairs but this time tea was taken in near silence. As we started to relax the Directing Staff appeared again and told us that we had more work to do.

We were given graph paper and told to prepare a large-scale section from an ordnance survey map. We worked in silence as the DS prowled around the room, stopping every so often to peer over someone's shoulder. Two hours later we were told that time had run out and we were allowed to return to our huts.

It was good to be able to take off my boots and I was thankful that I did not have any blisters. Leanne suddenly grabbed her towel and announced that she was going to have a bath. We all looked at each other and then there was a mad scramble as we all decided to do the same. Our damp kit was hung up in the hope that it might dry overnight, although no one really believed that it would. We each had two combat jackets and two pairs of trousers and we thought that we would have a psychological edge over the others if we could wear clean clothes. So it was decided that whenever anyone had some free time they would begin to handwash the kit. We could not stand the thought of having to wear filthy clothing for another two weeks.

Having made this decision, we all slept like logs that night. I was amazed and thankful that we had been allowed a full night of rest. The next morning after breakfast we stood in our ranks waiting for the next ordeal to begin. There were two hundred of us waiting and soon we were directed to an area where we could see two Land Rovers were parked.

The DS from the Paras climbed on to the bonnet of one of the Land Rovers and told us that we would be divided into two teams. He hoped that his team had the will to win, as he did not like to lose. Then he said, 'Today I am Ben Hur and you, scumbags, are my slaves.' Pointing to the Land Rover he said, 'This is my chariot.'

We split into our two teams and ropes were attached to each of the Land Rovers, on each of which sat a DS. They looked down on us as if they were gods. We took the strain on the ropes, someone yelled 'GO' and the race began. It was difficult to get into a proper rhythm and there was a lot of stumbling. No one took charge and our DS screamed at us to pull harder. One man in our team fell over but no one bothered about him. Later I discovered that he had been run over by the Land Rover and had broken his arm. No one gave him any sympathy; we did not have the time to think of anything but the task in hand. I could see that we were in the lead. Even so the DS was screaming at us to try harder. I began to pull harder but my hands were slipping on the rope. Then, suddenly, we were over the finishing line and we had won. Cheering, we fell into a heap. The unfortunate losers had to suffer a stream of verbal abuse and yet more push-ups.

The following day, after a PT session, my number was called out and I was told to change into civilian clothes. I stood around waiting with about eighty others for some transport to arrive.

Eventually a number of three-ton trucks pulled up and the DS shouted at us all to get into the back of them. We set off not knowing what we would have to do. The trucks made their way along narrow tracks, eventually coming to a stop by some buildings. A group of us were told to jump out and a DS came with us. The truck moved on.

We gathered around the DS, a quiet, good-looking man with stunning blue eyes. He handed us each a school graph book and told us to walk around the buildings and make notes of everything we saw. He particularly stressed that we should make accurate notes of the houses and amenities, as, when we returned to camp, we would have to prepare a scale map of the area. This was a task that I enjoyed. It was a warm, sunny day and it was good to wander around by myself without the DS harassing me.

As I walked through a field I glanced over and saw two of the Directing Staff sitting down. Each of them was enjoying a mug of tea and, as I went past, they raised their mugs to me. I just thought 'smug bastards' and carried on walking. The time we had been allotted soon ran out and we were loaded back into our truck and driven back to camp.

Once we were back in camp we sat down and began reproducing the area on large sheets of graph paper, adding all our own observations. A DS in Naval uniform came over to me and looked at the map. He studied it for a while and then said, 'It's not bad, but what about the power lines? Don't forget, detail is everything.' In my mind I retraced my steps, trying to remember where I had seen the power lines. Eventually the two hours that we had been given to complete the map came to an end and I was relieved that I had just about finished.

Thinking that the map-making had been the last task of the day, we settled down to sleep in our hut. Experience had taught us that it was best to sleep still dressed in our combat gear and we were thankful on this occasion that we had done so. We had not been in bed for long when the door to our hut was noisily flung open and a voice yelled out, 'Come on, ladies. Let's have you.' We fell out of bed and laced our boots, before running over to the hall.

In the hall we found that the chairs had again been arranged in rows with a screen placed in the front. My heart sank: not more documentaries about the uses of bamboo, surely? Pencils and paper were distributed and then the film began. This time, however, it was not bamboo but pictures of different weapons. Frame after frame showed weapons of all kinds and also weapon parts. I tried very hard to remember the lecture we had had on the subject and write down what they were. It was difficult. I was very tired and my brain seemed to be working in slow motion. At the end of the film the lights were put back on and we had to hand in our papers. This time they were not marked and we were allowed to return to our huts.

By now we were all wide awake. We knew that we would not get much sleep that night and so stretched out on our beds and talked. Most of the talk was about the directing staff and how we hated them. Then Lucy told us about one DS in particular who had been leering at her when she had to strip off to cross the river. The incident had really upset her and we lay on our beds in silence as she sobbed.

CHAPTER SIX

Over the next few days our numbers began to dwindle. The women were all still there but at least fifty men had gone by the end of the first week.

One evening towards the end of that week we were sitting, enjoying a cup of tea in the cookhouse, when Mr Sneer interrupted us. 'I do hope that everyone has had a nice day,' he said, looking round at us with a smirk on his face. He continued, 'We can't have you enjoying yourselves too much, can we? PT kit. Outside. MOVE!'

We leapt to our feet, chairs scraping along the floor, mugs of tea slopping on to the tables. Five minutes later, clad in PT kit, we were standing outside in the dark. It was freezing cold. We were divided into groups of four and taken into the lecture hall, one group at a time.

When it was my turn I found myself in front of the hunk with blue eyes.

'190, you have sixty seconds to study this route,' he said. 'You are here and your destination is here, a distance of two miles.'

I carefully studied the map in front of me for the sixty seconds I had been allocated. As I was about to leave, the hunk added, 'By the way, before you go you have to memorize this,' and he held up a card on which was written a four-line poem. I was slightly confused and so he explained that, not only did I have to find my way to the next checkpoint but that when I arrived there I had to recite the poem to whoever was manning the post. It made no sense to me at all but I put it out of my mind and concentrated on the route I would take. We were all given fluorescent vests to wear and we made our way into the training area. I began to run and found that I had memorized my route well. In no time I had reached the first checkpoint but I had completely forgotten the poem. I thought hard and then managed to say something. It was obviously not right as the DS looked at me in disgust and said, 'That's the biggest load of bollocks I've heard tonight, 190. Study your next route and get out of my sight!'

I ran on towards the next checkpoint and the rain set in. By the end of the exercise I had run through five checkpoints, learning a new poem at each. As I reached the finishing line I realized that I had passed quite a few of the others, but I was exhausted. We were ushered into the cookhouse where we were given mugs of tea or hot chocolate and then we stood, waiting for the next task. Eventually one of the DS turned to a group of us and asked, 'Don't you lot want to go to bed?' I did not need to be told twice and headed for my hut and a hot bath.

The following evening we were again told to put on PT kit and assemble outside the cookhouse. I was dreading the thought of having to do another run and my body ached from all the physical exertion of the previous week. This time, however, we were led into the cookhouse, where a large square of mats had been put on the stage. The Training Major stood up and announced that we should prepare to take part in the noble art of milling. I did not understand what he meant and whispered to Leanne, 'What is he talking about?' I soon discovered that milling is another term for boxing. I was shocked. I knew that the men boxed but I had never heard of women being made to fight before. This was a very primitive form of boxing. The contestants were not evenly matched and they were not interested in style. All that was required was that you beat your opponent to a pulp.

The first match began: three rounds, each one minute long. One of the contestants was much shorter that the other and he went down in the first round, his nose smashed and bloodied. He was pulled out of the ring by the medics who patched him up. His opponent waved his arms in the air and we all cheered. As each fight progressed the atmosphere began to affect us and before long we were all enthusiastically shouting and cheering.

Suddenly I heard, '190 and 128' shouted out by the referee, a small, wiry Para with untidy blond hair. I looked around and saw the other girls staring back at me. Once again the numbers were called and I stood up and stepped into the ring at the same time as Liz. By now the room was silent as Liz and I stood in opposite corners staring at each other. I had never hit anyone before and had no desire to start now, but there was no way out. My heart began thumping as the boxing gloves were put on to my outstretched hands and then the bell rang.

I stood looking at Liz as she rushed towards me, gloved hands raised to protect her face. I hoped that she would hit me first so that I would not feel so guilty about retaliating. Before a single punch was thrown the referee reached out and grabbed Liz, pulling her out of the ring. I stood there, hands at my sides not knowing what I was supposed to do next. The DS were looking at each other, knowing smiles on their faces and when I turned to the referee I could see why. To my horror, he was putting boxing gloves on himself. Before I had the chance to protest the bell rang and he came towards me, hissing through clenched teeth, 'Come on girly. Now's your chance.'

I threw a weak punch and was rewarded with a cuff on the ear. It stung and I could see the referee smiling down at me. From the side of the ring the crowd began to roar, 'Kill him!' I did not know how to box but knew that if I were not careful I would be injured. In an instant I decided what had to be done. I charged and hit the referee with my shoulder. As I made contact I punched him in the groin. I felt his body sag and he slid towards the floor. On the edge of the ring the crowd was going mad, shouting and cheering. They hoisted me on to someone's shoulders and paraded me in front of the Directing Staff, who were looking at the entire scene in astonishment. Some of them were actually laughing. The Training Major grudgingly gave me a 'thumbs up'. In the ring the referee was still writhing around the floor, purple-faced and clutching himself. One – nil to us!

The following morning as we made our way to breakfast everyone was talking about my victory. We reached the cookhouse and were surprised to see that the shutters were still closed.

They did not remain closed for long. As they rolled up we saw that the Directing Staff were standing behind the counter. 'Morning, campers,' they chorused. 'Breakfast will be served al fresco this morning. Outside, MOVE!'

We went outside and the DS who had acted as referee the night before came up to me. 'I don't like you, 190,' he said, 'and I've decided that I'm going to hurt you.'

Having delivered this threat he moved away and we set off, at the double, for the assault course. I completed my first circuit and returned to the start, breathing heavily. The referee, who was by now accompanied by the tall Para with the moustache, met me. They both looked very pleased with themselves and offered me breakfast. They produced a large pot full of porridge. I declined but they insisted that I eat and pushed a ladle into my face. I struggled to eat the gluey mess. As soon as I had finished they sent me off around the assault course again. This time it was more difficult, my legs and arms were aching and I had not realized how physically tired I had become with all the exercise I had been taking. On my return, as I stood gasping for breath, the Para again came over and ordered me to eat some more porridge. By now I had to make a great effort not to be sick. Another mouthful and they sent me off again to do another circuit. I passed some of the others who were retching uncontrollably, and finally gave in myself and was sick. Through the waves of nausea I could hear the Directing Staff sneering, 'Just like a woman. No guts!'

By now I was on the verge of tears but was determined not to give in. I set off on the circuit again and soon came to the six-foot wall. It was a tough obstacle at the best of times but now, in my weakened state, I found it impossible. I frantically clawed at it but was unable to get a hold until suddenly I felt myself being pushed over the top. I rolled over and landed on the ground on the other side. Next to me fell the man who had helped me over. He pulled me to my feet and said kindly, 'Come on, love, you're almost there.' Then he took my arm and ran with me to the finish.

I stood gasping for breath, determined not to fall over. The Directing Staff came over to me and, instead of the confrontation I had expected, they merely said, 'That's enough, 190. Get changed and we'll see you again in one hour.' I was confused and felt quite deflated, having psyched myself up for some more abuse. All around me the medics were working on numerous cases of sickness and twisted ankles. Everyone was exhausted.

By now there were only ten women left. While the lads went off to set up and man observation posts around the area we were taken by Dennis the Menace for more weapon training. I knew that time was now running out and that I had to be more than proficient in order to pass.

We were called over to the range individually. On the ground was a tarpaulin and when it was my turn I was told that underneath it was a self-loading rifle which I had to strip and reassemble against the clock. As an afterthought I was told that I must perform the task wearing a blindfold.

As soon as I was given the go ahead to begin, I felt around under the tarpaulin until my hands touched the rifle and then I began to strip it. I managed it quite easily and sat up when I had finished. I was still wearing the blindfold and I could hear the DS pulling back the tarpaulin. He inspected the rifle and said, 'Hmm, not bad. Now reassemble it.' This was much more difficult than stripping it and I groped about trying to find all the small parts and slot them into place. Suddenly I heard a hissing noise and froze, completely disorientated. The noise stopped to be replaced immediately by a loud bang. I threw myself forward on to the ground and heard the DS laughing, 'Too slow, 190. We thought you needed a rocket up your arse.'

I tore off my blindfold and found an empty flashbang shell behind me. My only thought was, 'I wish I had a loaded gun in front of me so I could shoot this bastard.'

Later that evening while the men were still away at their observation posts the women were paired up and sent out on an orienteering exercise. My partner was Liz and we were given a map, a compass and a route and were told to, 'Fuck off and don't get lost.'

We ran off into the darkness, across ploughed fields, being careful not to rush and injure ourselves. Navigating in the dark was difficult, especially as the terrain was unfamiliar to us. We had to trust our compass bearings. There were no easy points of reference such as church spires and I was becoming so paranoid about the whole thing that I even double-checked all the signs on the footpaths in case the DS had changed them around. Finally we completed our task without mishap and returned to the waiting Directing Staff who were sitting in a Land Rover.

As we approached, the tall Para got out and came over to us. 'Nice one, ladies,' he remarked, 'there's tea for you in the back.' The warm, sweet tea was really welcome and, after we had drunk it, Liz and I sat in the back of the Land Rover, hugging the tea urn in an attempt to defrost our cold fingers and toes.

Within an hour most of the other women had returned. We began to compare notes about the exercise. It seemed that most had had some difficulties such as being chased by farm dogs or falling over gates. We laughed about Leanne who had had her backside stung by a nettle whilst paying a call of nature.

Suddenly someone said, 'Has anyone seen 80 and 124?' Everyone stopped talking. It seemed that no one knew what had happened to either of them. I looked over at the DS and could see the luminous dial of his watch. It was two-thirty am. I suddenly felt very tired and ached all over.

The Para was becoming agitated and informed us that none of us was going anywhere until the other two had been found. A second Land Rover had arrived and we were split between the two. The Para revved the engine of our Land Rover and the wheels spun as we went off to search for the missing girls. We drove round and round the country roads, the DS becoming more and more agitated as time passed. Eventually we heard the magic words, 'Found them,' over the radio and we all relaxed.

We arrived back in camp in time to see the girls being shouted at by one of the DS. Not content to leave it to his colleague, the Para who had been driving our Land Rover leapt out and rushed over to add his own words of abuse. The rest of us were told to assemble the next morning at nine am in full combat gear and with full water bottles. 'Next morning' actually meant a few hours later and we staggered off to bed, grateful for whatever sleep we might get in what remained of the night.

The men returned from their observation posts and at nine am we all assembled, as instructed, and waited for the inspection by the DS. They walked up and down our lines checking that our water bottles had been filled to the brim. Anyone who had not done so was reprimanded. A convoy of four-ton trucks arrived and, after we had been issued with maps and compasses, our numbers were called out and we were ordered into the trucks. I found myself squashed between two hefty men.

Some of the others were talking among themselves and it seemed that they knew what was in store for us. A young man sitting opposite me looked up and smiled. 'It's a fair old yomp today,' he said. I knew from this slang term that he must be a Marine; only Marines refer to a long walk as a 'yomp'. I asked him how long he thought it would take and he grinned, 'All day, I should think.'

After a while the truck stopped and a DS appeared at the back and called out two numbers. They scrambled out of the truck and huddled around him with their maps. A minute or so later they turned and jogged away from the truck. The DS climbed on board again and we resumed our journey. The next stop was in the middle of some old buildings and this time it was my number that was called, along with that of a young lad. The DS pointed out on our maps exactly where we were and then told us where he wanted us to go. We were given grid references, but they were not the same, so I knew I would not have company on the next part of the exercise. As I checked my reference I heard the truck pulling away and looked up to see the friendly Marine smiling at me from the back and giving me a thumbs up.

I made a quick calculation and estimated that I was about four miles away from the next checkpoint. The best route seemed to be via footpaths and I set off at a jog. For the first mile it was easy, although my legs ached from the physical exertion of the past two weeks. Then I came to a large ploughed field. I started to cross it but soon realized that I had not picked the best route at all. My boots soon became clogged with mud, making it difficult to walk and I kept slipping in the furrows. My water bottle was strapped around my waist and kept banging against me. It irritated me so much that I emptied out the water.

Eventually I reached the other side of the field and stopped to scrape the mud from my boots. I knew that I had wasted valuable time and so set off again along the road at a fast pace. The extra effort made me thirsty and I realized what a fool I had been to throw away all the water. Everything was going wrong and I found it difficult to concentrate on what I had to do. At last I reached the first checkpoint and found two DS sitting on the tailgate of the Land Rover. One of them looked at me and enquired, 'What kept you, 190?' He gave me a grid reference for the next checkpoint and asked me to point it out to him on the map. I set off again at a run and heard him shouting, 'Have a nice day!'

The next leg was easier or would have been if I had not now been suffering from a raging thirst. I again cursed myself for my stupidity but had no choice but to continue. I came to some more buildings and stopped for a moment to check my map and to catch my breath. Suddenly I could sense that I was being watched and turned to see a man peering at me from behind a wall. The man walked up to me and pointed down the road. Then he looked at me and said, 'Your friends have gone that way, young lady.' I asked if he would be kind enough to let me have some water and held out my muddy water bottle. He took it and held it as if he thought it might be contaminated while he filled it from a nearby tap. He looked me up and down and asked who I was. I told him I was in the Army and that I was on an exercise. He looked at me with obvious distaste and then shook his head, muttering, 'But they look so smart on the television!'

I thanked him for the water and made my way towards a DS I could see waiting in the distance. I collected my next set of co-ordinates from the DS and set off once more. This time my route took me through some forestry. I was nervous, as I knew how easy it was to get lost in woodland. It was quiet and dark and I took a compass bearing before plunging into the thick undergrowth. As I had expected there were a number of tracks and I found it hard to follow the footpath. I stopped several times to check my compass. I was becoming very tired as I had already covered eight or nine miles. My concentration was slipping and I suddenly tripped over something and fell. My ankle began to throb and I saw that I had caught my foot in the roots of a tree. Not for the first time that day I cursed my stupidity, but my anger soon turned to despair. I managed to stand but knew that I would no longer be able to run or even walk properly and I still had to get out of the woods and on to the next checkpoint.

I was thankful that my boots and the puttees I was also wearing gave my ankle some support. I found a squashed Mars bar in my pocket and, having devoured it, felt a lot better. The pain in my ankle had subsided to a constant dull ache and I was able to hobble along, eventually reaching the next checkpoint.

The DS could see that I was limping and asked if I wanted to give up. I told him I did not and was subjected to more ignorant abuse. He told me that he was sick of the women who were always either bleeding or bleating and concluded with, 'If it's sympathy you want, you can kiss my arse.'

I was so fed up with this abuse that I could easily have turned on him but I knew that it would do me no good and managed to bite my tongue. Insults and ill treatment were regarded as perfectly legitimate behaviour for the DS but would never have been tolerated by the Army had the trainees behaved in the same way.

I was offered a cup of tea which I gratefully accepted. I drank the hot sweet brew in silence, my body shaking with fatigue. It was now mid-afternoon and the temperature had begun to drop.

The next section of the exercise was all uphill and I could see figures in front of me, running up the steep slopes and across fields. I could no longer run but dragged myself as best I could to the next checkpoint, arriving after dark. The DS regarded me without sympathy and asked for my map. I produced the tatty, mud-spattered Ordnance Survey map and he ordered me to do twenty press-ups for not looking after it.

I dropped to the ground and began. I had only completed two when I felt a hand on my collar, pulling me up again. It was the same DS, telling me not to waste time and pointing out with his torch where I would find the next checkpoint. I glanced at the map and my heart sank when I saw that it was at least five miles away. I started to walk and then heard the DS shout, 'Double!' and tried to run. By now I was exhausted and tears ran down my face, dripping off my chin. Ahead I could see the silhouette of someone moving towards me and recognized the voice of the sarcastic Para, calling me over to him. I pulled my cap down to hide my tears and stood before him, wondering what torture he had in mind for me this time. He only said, 'Get in the truck, 190.' I knew that this would mean the end and I refused. He would not allow me a choice and said, 'Get in the bloody truck. I know you're thick, but this is it – *finito*.'

I felt sick and the sense of failure was overwhelming. I could just about make out the shape of the truck and walked round to the back of it, where a number of hands stretched out and pulled me on board. The journey back to camp was silent, everyone lost in his own thoughts. We were told to assemble again in the morning at seven am and were advised to go straight to bed.

Back in the hut my first thought was for a bath. Most of the others were already back and had discovered that there was no hot water. I pulled off my boots and socks and was shocked by the condition of my ankle, which was swollen and bruised. I ran a bath in spite of the water temperature and lay back, watching the tepid water turn to a muddy brown.

The next morning we assembled as instructed and were greeted by the Training Major, who was accompanied by the DS. He told us that he would call out some numbers and that, if we heard our own number, we should go immediately to the canteen. He consulted his clipboard and then began the roll call. Nervously I waited. The list of numbers went on and on; 172, 183, 204. Suddenly I realized that my number would not be called and I was filled with an indescribable sense of failure and disappointment. I could hardly believe that I had gone through all that mental and physical abuse only to be passed over right at the end of the training.

The roll call came to an end. There were thirty of us still standing in silence waiting to learn our fate. The Training Major cleared his throat and looked at the forlorn little bunch of volunteers; then he spoke. 'Right, you lot. I expect to see you all at midday on Monday for the next phase. Staff, take them away and brief them.' The atmosphere turned from one of despondency to that of euphoria. I looked around and saw Leanne waving to me. Julia, Kate and Liz were also still there. We had made it after all.

Mr Sneer began his briefing. He told us that we were all a bunch of losers and that we were very lucky to have got this far. Then he said that the next phase would last for five months and that we would be going to a training camp I had never heard of. He reminded us that we were not permitted to talk to anyone about the training and told us not to forget to be back at midday the following Monday.

By the time the briefing finished and we got back to our hut the other girls were leaving. There was an awkwardness between us now. No one knew what to say and so we all finished our packing in silence.

CHAPTER SEVEN

I went home for the weekend, dragging a case that was filled with dirty washing. Mum wanted to know what I had been doing as she had not heard from me for over two weeks. All I could tell her was that I had made it through to the next stage of my training. She asked what would happen next and I said that I had no idea. I am sure that she thought I was lying to her but she did not push me for an answer. She even refrained from commenting when she opened my suitcase to take out my washing and the smell from my filthy clothes knocked her backwards.

It was good to be home but I still had some things to do. After Mr Sneer's briefing, one of the WRAC sergeants had told us that we would need a lot of civilian clothing. She told us to make sure that we had a variety of clothes and that they should be loose-fitting. I spent most of that Saturday choosing new clothes and shoes. They cost me a fortune. On Sunday I had to iron my kit and re-pack my case and, almost before I realized it, the weekend was over.

On Monday morning I struggled down to the railway station, this time burdened by two suitcases and a sports bag, and caught my train. At the station I met up with Leanne, who was waiting for me in her car. It was my job to navigate to our training camp, which was not shown on any map. As we drove along the road we came to a section with high fences on either side. We continued for about a mile and then, through the trees on the right, we could just make out an assault course. According to our instructions we were nearly there and so Leanne slowed the car and there, in front of us, we could see the gatehouse.

As we turned in at the gate we spotted some MOD police behind a thick, reinforced glass window. They were staring back at us and eventually one of them came to the window and asked, 'Can I help you?' We showed him our warrant cards and gave him our names. He went back into the gatehouse and returned with a list on a clipboard, on which he checked our details. Once he was satisfied that we were who we said we were, the barrier was raised and we drove into the camp. I was surprised to see that it was quite modern.

We made our way to the reception area and were met by the same support staff who had greeted us when we arrived at Camp Alpha. This time they were much more polite and showed us to the female block where we would be staying. It was in the same building as the DS accommodation although it was one floor above. We still had to share, four to a room, but the rooms were large with wonderful views of the surrounding countryside, so it was much more pleasant than our previous accommodation. The rest of the camp was fairly compact. Our rooms were a short distance from the dining room, next to which was the lecture hall and classroom.

Julia was the only officer in our room and she found it very strange having to share. She tried to pull rank and organize us but Leanne tactfully told her to shut up.

By midday the others had all arrived and we stood around nervously, waiting for the course to begin. We did not know what to expect, although, having been screamed at and generally abused for the past two weeks, we were sure we would not be in for an easy time. No one was quite prepared for what followed.

We were ushered into the lecture hall and everyone made a mad scramble for the seats at the back as none of us wanted to appear to be too keen by sitting at the front. The seats were tiered and, as we looked down from the back, the door below us opened and in walked the Training Major, followed by the Directing Staff we had all grown to hate. Looking round at us the Training Major said, 'Welcome to your new home. You have met most of my staff. However, I think the time has come for us to introduce ourselves properly.' As he finished speaking the majority of the DS removed their familiar berets and replaced them with a variety of different berets including sandy-coloured berets bearing the winged dagger emblem of the SAS. There was a stunned silence.

Like most of the others, the closest I thought I had come to this legendary regiment was watching the television pictures of the storming of the Iranian Embassy. Now I realized I had been wrong.

The Major was speaking again. 'You are all volunteers,' he said, 'Most of you will not be successful.' He paused and glanced around the room, a disdainful look on his face. 'Your instructors have all been hand-picked so if they tell you to do something, you do it. Clear?' As one, we replied, 'Yes, Sir!' and the Training Major marched out, followed by most of the DS.

My mind was racing. Could this be one of their mind games? I decided it must be genuine. There would be no point in it being a game.

Only three DS now remained: the blonde WRAC sergeant, Mr Sneer and the Major's right-hand man, who was a powerfully built Northerner. He was one of those who was wearing the SAS beret and the insignia of a warrant officer. Mr Sneer addressed us, 'You'll be pleased to know that you are no longer numbers. You can use Christian names now, either your own or one you have made up. It doesn't matter either way. While you are here you must not discuss your background with anyone at all. The less you know about each other the better for all of you. If one of you were to be captured, we wouldn't want you squealing about your colleagues, would we?'

Mr Sneer droned on and on. The rules and regulations here were just as rigid as they had been at Camp Alpha; mail would be vetted, phone calls monitored and we would have no free time off camp. There was a bar that we could use on the camp but we were told it would be preferable if we only had soft drinks.

When Mr Sneer finished speaking we were taken to the armoury, where we were each issued with a 9mm pistol, two rounds of blank ammunition and a leather clip-on holster. We were instructed to load the pistol and cock the weapon to ensure that there was a round up the spout. We had to take our pistols everywhere we went, even to bed. If anyone was caught without it or it was not properly loaded there would be a fine to pay. Being left-handed I had anticipated some problems with the safety catch so I was surprised to find that the safety catch on my pistol was for a left-handed person. It felt very strange to have to carry around a loaded pistol, as the issue of weapons was normally very strictly controlled.

We were split into two groups, one to start the course with a week of driving assessment and the other to learn about photography. My group started with the photography but not until we had all been taken for a run around the camp. This was conducted by the DS we had come to know as Bruce Forsyth but who now introduced himself as Ted. We were accompanied on the run by Ted's dog, Gnasher, an aggressive Rottweiler. Ted had taught this fearsome creature to knock over trainees and pin them to the ground, growling as he stood guard. Ted found this very amusing. During that first run, Gnasher attacked me, grabbing my arm in his massive jaws. Ted called him off saying, 'Now then Gnasher, you don't want to spoil your tea, do you?'

The area around the camp was enormous and we ran on the only road, a distance of about three miles. The area was littered with signs of the specialist training that took place here: a passenger aircraft which, we were told, was used by the regiment to practise hostage release and a mock-up of an embassy building, used in much the same way. We also passed huge earthworks that were used for firing practise and there was, of course, the dreaded assault course.

The walls of the mock embassy were white but had been stained black by the numerous stun grenades that had been hurled at them. As we ran past we suddenly had to scatter to allow through two white Range Rovers that showed no sign of stopping. Each carried a group of men dressed in black, their faces obscured by camouflage paint.

We carried on running and soon came to a straight stretch of road in sight of the camp buildings. Ted shouted for the women to continue running and the men to stop. Then, after about ten seconds, he ordered the men to catch up with us. From behind we could hear the pounding of feet as the men gained on us. We ran faster but they soon caught up and Ted screamed at us all to go faster and faster. Eventually we collapsed, gasping, at the gates. As I lay there trying to catch my breath I suddenly noticed a gaggle of geese bearing down upon us at speed. Their necks were extended and they were hissing like demented snakes. They came to a stop a few feet away from us and stood, honking and flapping their wings. Ted thought it was very funny that we had been penned in by a flock of birds.

The next day I began my crash course in photography. The studio was a small, cramped building that reeked of chemicals and our instructor was a fat Sergeant from the Intelligence Corps. He issued each of us with a Nikon SLR FE2 camera and a variety of lenses. We spent the day learning about depth of field, focal length, camera lenses and lighting. I had never had an interest in photography and by the end of the day my head was spinning. We were issued with some black and white films and told to go out and practise what we had learnt. So much of the area was out of bounds that our subject matter was limited. I wandered off towards the car park taking pictures of anything and everything. The geese came in for a lot of attention but they eventually got fed up with it and chased us off.

Once the films had all been used we went back to the studio for our first lesson in developing. Fifteen of us crowded into the developing room, tripping over each other as we wound the film on to spools, then developed, stopped and fixed the film. We were all eager to see how we had done. In the infra-red light of the studio I was amazed as I watched images appearing on the photographic paper. It was exhilarating to see the results of our work and most of us quickly became hooked on photography.

We learned to use a variety of different lenses and to take photos in poor light. Then we tackled infra-red photography. We stood in a circle in the developing room, a pile of spools in the centre. The flashes on our cameras had been covered with an infra-red film and we focused on the pile of spools with the aid of a torch. Once we were all ready the torches were extinguished and we took our photographs.

For our next lesson, the torches were covered with the infra-red film and their light could only be seen with the aid of night vision goggles. It was difficult trying to focus the camera whilst wearing these goggles and the light from the torches glowed eerily in the eyepiece. We practised this technique time and time again before we felt comfortable with it. We were told that in a real situation we would have to take photos with infra-red cameras, as any light that was used would pinpoint our positions and put us in danger.

Towards the end of the course we learnt about taking photos covertly in hostile areas. We were shown a tiny camera that could be hidden almost anywhere. These were referred to as James Bond spy cameras. The tall, blonde WRAC sergeant, who we now knew as Nina, gave all the women some ideas as to how they could be effective.

I was given a shoulder bag and told to conceal a camera in it. I found it was easy to hide the camera inside and keep it steady with foam packaging and Velcro straps. Taking a photo with the hidden camera was much more difficult. The basic idea was to walk towards the target, point the bag in the right direction and click the switch. In reality it was difficult to walk naturally and turn the bag in the right direction without attracting attention. We practised for a long while and took some fine shots of knees or the sky, rarely managing to focus on the face of the target. Eventually I found that the best way to carry the bag was under my arm rather than on my shoulder. I angled it slightly upwards so that, when I turned, the lens was pointing in the right direction.

For our next lesson we were shown how to conceal and use a camera in a car. It was a tricky business, trying to find the best angle to take the best picture as you sat there, without being noticed. Most cars were fitted with a prestle switch, or tiny button, that was positioned beside the driver. When it was pressed it activated a motor drive which took a series of photographs. Terrorists going about their daily lives are sometime photographed in this way as it usually provides the security forces with good quality pictures of both them and their associates.

Leanne had been put in the other group and had spent her first week on the driving course. Each evening we would meet in the bar and discuss what we had done that day. I began to dread the driving course. Leanne was an experienced driver but even she had found it very difficult. I had only been driving for a few weeks, so knew I was in for a rough time.

The second week began and we were divided into teams of three with one DS to each team. I was put in a team with two men, Jack and Andy, and our instructor who was called Mike. He was the same soft-spoken man with the gorgeous smile and stunning blue eyes who had handed out the graph books on our map-making exercise.

The first morning was spent checking over the cars. We had a pool of assorted high-powered Mazdas, Toyotas and Vauxhalls which, we were told, had all been used in Northern Ireland. For one reason or another they had been compromised and so had been shipped back to be thrashed by trainees. Inside each car were a number of tiny holes, almost invisible against the black of the car interior. These holes were where the prestle switches for the radio equipment and hidden cameras had been fitted. Mike told us that we would be responsible for the cars, checking oil and water levels in the morning and refuelling and washing them each evening. He stressed that we were not to drive fast in the small roads surrounding the camp, as it was important not to upset the locals or draw attention to ourselves.

Dave then told us to get into our car. Jack and I climbed into the back and Andy sat in the front as Mike drove us out of the camp. He went at a steady speed for about two miles until we had left the local lanes behind and had reached the main road. Then he pulled away at the junction, engaged second gear and floored the accelerator. The car responded immediately and Mike kept his foot on the floor as he smoothly changed gears, overtaking every car he came to. For the next thirty minutes Mike put the car through its paces, hurtling along the country lanes and never seeming to get out of third gear. Then he pulled over and, turning back towards Jack and me, said, 'It's as simple as that!'

I was picked to drive first. I was very nervous. I had only ever driven a Chevette and it was nowhere near as responsive or fast as the car I now had to drive. I pushed the seat as far forward as it would go and folded my jacket to use as a cushion to give me a bit more height. Then I sat, wondering what I should do next. Mike said 'Right, let's go.' I took a deep breath and, silently saying to myself, 'mirror, signal, and manoeuvre', pulled away. I drove at a very sedate pace, working my way up through the gears. Mike yelled at me, 'Floor it', but by now I was in fourth gear and when I put my foot down the car was very sluggish. 'Third,' shouted Mike.

I was becoming very flustered and crunched the gears. In my mirror I could see Jack and Andy lurch forward as the car pulled away. The speed shocked me. I was approaching a tight bend and began to brake as I steered towards it. Too late I realized that the car had power steering as we skidded sideways, brakes locked. Jack and Andy were screaming at me to pull over and Mike yelled, 'Get your foot off the brake!' The car shuddered to a halt and we sat for a moment in silence. Then Mike said quietly, 'Start her up and pull over there.'

I parked in the lay-by that he had indicated and he told me to get out. He demanded to know if I had ever passed a driving test. I told him that I had only had about two weeks' experience from scratch and had passed my test just before coming on the course. My face was burning with embarrassment.

Mike took a deep breath before saying quietly, 'You have got to pass this phase to be able to carry on. You and I have got a lot of work to do. Listen to what I say, do it without question and we might get you through. OK?' I nodded and climbed back into the driving seat. I squirmed as, from the back seat, I heard Jack mutter, 'Women drivers!' Immediately Mike rounded on him saying, 'One more word from you and you're history! This course is about teamwork and if that is too difficult for you then it's time for you to leave.'

I started the engine once more and Mike began a commentary, telling me exactly what he wanted me to do. I followed each instruction, concentrating so hard that by the time we stopped half an hour later I was drenched in sweat and my hands ached from gripping the steering wheel. I climbed into the back seat and it was Jack's turn.

Jack was still smarting from Mike's earlier comment and drove off at breakneck speed. When his time was up he pulled over and I could see him looking at me in his rear view mirror, a smug look on his face. Mike looked at him and began his appraisal. By the time he had finished telling Jack that his performance was dangerous, reckless and, at times, out of control, the smug look had disappeared.

My confidence began to grow. Each day we drove a different vehicle and, although I knew I was not as good as the majority of the trainees, I was improving. On the final day we each had to take a one-hour test. I had to pass it to stay on the course. I knew how happy Jack would be if I failed. Mike told me to concentrate and to listen to what the DS said. The three of us drew lots to see who would go first. It was Andy, then Jack; I came last. My assessor was Mr Sneer, whom we now knew as John. As I got into the car I saw Jack waving at me. 'Patronising bastard,' I thought before turning my attention to the test.

The hour passed very quickly. I had to give John a running commentary on what I was doing which was good as it helped me to concentrate. He asked a few questions about signs that we had passed or car registrations to see if I was able to concentrate on more than one thing at a time. At the end of the hour we sat and debriefed.

As usual John showed no emotion as he told me that I drove like a man with a flat cap, in a Morris Minor, on a Sunday afternoon. Then he said that I was safe and observant and that he was willing to give me the benefit of the doubt. I had passed!

The second week of the course was over and we had all managed to get through it. We sat around in the cookhouse, wondering what would happen next. Suddenly the DS started shouting at us to produce our weapons. The DS at my table was called Harry and I immediately pulled up my jumper to show him that I was carrying my pistol. He told me to unload it so I took the magazine off and cocked the slide back to eject the round in the breech. Harry took a moment to congratulate me before pouncing on Julian who, we were all sure, was an officer. He did not have his weapon on him and, instead of admitting it, tried to bluff his way out. Harry was not fooled for a moment and told Julian that he was being fined a fiver for bullshitting. That was when the fines book was started. Each fine was noted in the book and the money went towards paying for an end-of-course party for those who were successful. I just hoped that I would still be there at the end to enjoy it.

CHAPTER EIGHT

The next phase of the training was a two-week intensive close-quarter battle course, or CQB for short. It was during this course that we learnt what to do with the weapons we had all been carrying. The instructors for this part of the training were mostly from the SAS and the chief instructor was an Australian called Brian.

Each day we were packed into two transit vans and driven to the firing range. It was the strangest place I had ever seen. It was twenty-five metres long and was enclosed by high earth walls. At one end there were six targets and at the other a wooden hut that was just big enough for us all to squeeze into if it rained. Apart from the hut there was nothing else there. Calls of nature were taken behind bushes outside the range. Twice a day an urn filled with hot tea was brought to us from the camp. The training began with a demonstration by the instructors. We were hanging around drinking our tea when I heard the sound of a car engine coming from outside the range. Two of the men, Vince and Ben, were standing at the entrance when suddenly a silver Toyota appeared from nowhere. They had to dive out of the way, tea spilling everywhere, as the car hurtled into view. The far end of the range erupted in flames and there was a sudden rush of warm air as the explosive wave hit us. Amid the screeching of brakes and rapid firing, the car doors flew open and out tumbled four men, fanning out along the range. There was constant firing as each man then worked his way back to the car, a few metres at a time. Suddenly it was all over. I was amazed at how quickly everything had happened. We were taken to look at the targets, each of which represented a human figure. The head and chest area of each of them was covered in 9mm bullet holes.

Brian gathered us together and told us that by the end of our training we would be able to shoot with that accuracy in our sleep. He also told us that we would be able to kill without thinking. It would be a gut reaction and if we did stop to think it would be too late; we would be shot first. He actually used the term 'slotted', which I discovered was SAS slang for 'shot', as was 'banjoed'. Brian called incoming rounds 'little red hornets'.

The start of our training covered very basic things like drawing a weapon. We had to stand six in a line, legs slightly apart, hands tensed by our sides waiting for the order to draw. When it came we pushed aside our jackets and grabbed for the butt of the pistol, thrusting the weapon forward and, at the same time, bringing up the other hand to support it. Sometimes, in our haste to do well, the pistol came flying out of someone's pocket and landed somewhere down the range. It was not as easy as it looked.

We learnt some tricks like putting a stone or some other heavy weight into the pocket or lining of a coat or jacket. This was done to make it easier to move clothing out of the way, allowing quick access to the weapon, and we spent an entire day practising. As Brian had told us, this had to become second nature to each of us. Ideally we should be able to draw and engage a target in less than two seconds.

At the end of the practice day we were allowed to load our weapons and shoot at the targets. We were taught the technique of 'double tapping' or aiming two rapid shots at the chest of the target. This was thought to be the best method of obtaining a kill. At the very least, two rapid shots that hit anywhere would put a terrorist out of action. If the shots were aimed correctly they should hit the target within a couple of inches of each other. This technique worked well at close range. Once a target was more than twenty yards away a single shot was preferable. At that distance double tapping was often inaccurate.

We spent days practising. At first we faced the targets and fired on command. As we progressed we stood side-on from both left and right and, on the command, turned and fired. Then we fired while walking towards the targets, which could be electronically activated. We repeated this time and again. In the end we could walk the length of the range and, hearing the targets move behind us, turn as one and take them out. I was astonished at how quickly I became conditioned to reacting in a certain way. I found that I was firing instinctively. There was no time to aim; I kept both eyes open and just focused on the body mass in front of me. It had always been assumed that female wrists were too weak to control a weapon. However, the recoil on a 9mm was minimal and the women performed well; our shots were as accurate as those of the men. The days spent on the range were long and exhausting, but I was never bored.

The second week we were introduced to car drills. These drills were to simulate ambush situations that could occur in remote country areas of Northern Ireland. They were supposed to give us a taste of what could happen so that if we encountered the real thing we would be prepared. Terrorists sometimes set up illegal vehicle checkpoints or IVCPs. Having stopped a car, they then had to approach it, which was when our training would take over.

The cars with which we practised had been used in Northern Ireland by other operators. They had either been compromised or had come to the end of their working life and most were battered and bullet-ridden. None of the cars was fitted with a windscreen.

For our first exercises we drove onto the range, two of us in each car. A shot was fired which was the signal for the exercise to start. The object was to move as quickly as possible to the back of the range whilst giving each other cover. This was called fire and manoeuvre and it was not as easy as it seemed. We were constantly told to count our rounds. Anyone who did not could suddenly find himself out of ammunition. Then there would be an embarrassing pause while the culprit frantically tried to pull off the empty magazine, a situation made worse by the inevitable stream of abuse from the DS.

Counting rounds had to become second nature. Failure to do so in a live situation would mean almost certain death. Each magazine held fourteen rounds – fifteen, including the one up the spout. They had to be changed after seven double taps and we were told that under no circumstances were we to discard an empty magazine. There was no excuse to leave anything behind for the enemy.

We progressed to four in a car. This was much more dangerous. On the signal to stop, the driver and the front passenger would get out of the car and fan out while being covered by the rear passengers. They would then leave the car while being covered by the driver and front passenger. We would then cover each other alternately. It was difficult within the narrow confines of the range. As each pair crossed over they would often get into the line of fire of the other pair. Sometimes our shots hit the car and we were fined for each additional hole in the bodywork.

During one such practice I had stopped to refill my magazine when a car, driven by Ben, came roaring in and screeched to a halt. Mike and Vince burst out of the back and Julian, in front, began laying down fire. I had my back to the car and was wearing ear defenders. Suddenly I heard a muffled cry of 'Man down, man down,' and turned to see Julian, face down on the ground. There was a stunned silence and no one moved.

Ben was the first to react. He holstered his weapon and rushed over to Julian, turning him on to his side. Vince began to call for a medic as Julian coughed and a stream of blood erupted from his mouth. Our medic was called Nigel and every day he came out to the range with us and sat in a green army ambulance. I frantically looked around for Nigel but he was not there. Vince recoiled as the blood hit his leg, but no one else moved. We were rooted to the spot with shock. Brian and Bruce emerged from the hut at the end of the range. They walked so slowly and were so cool that at first I thought they had not seen what had happened. Brian glanced at Julian who was by now cradled in Ben's arms, his face covered with blood. Then he turned to us and said, 'What a fine bunch of blokes you are, leavin' yer mate to die.' Turning back to Julian he said, 'Git up mate.' Julian opened his eyes and got to his feet. We were stunned. Brian continued his lecture. 'If one of those little red hornets gets yer, I'm not going to be there for yer, nor is Nigel. You depend on each other; look out for each other and don't leave yer mate to die in the gutter, you yella bastards!'

We were still in shock, realizing that we had been conned, but also that we had reacted very badly, standing around like lost sheep. If Julian really had been hurt we would not have been any help to him at all. Then Nigel arrived in the ambulance and told us to be in the lecture hall that night for a lesson in battle trauma.

The lesson began with a video showing a number of injuries sustained in Vietnam. I watched in horrified fascination. This was the first time I had ever seen the damage a bullet can cause. We were shown a tiny wound in the chest caused by a two-inch bullet. When the body was turned over the exit wound was huge, most of the back having been blown away. Dum Dum bullets also caused horrible injuries. These were bullets that had been tampered with; usually the head of the bullet had had an X cut into the top. In its weakened state it disintegrated on impact. We learned that the Armalite rifle bullet would tip and tumble in flight and that when it hit flesh it would continue to tumble, literally ripping the inside of the body to shreds. The Armalite was a favourite weapon for terrorists. The bullets of high-velocity rifles will penetrate bricks. It did not take much imagination to realize what they would do to the human body and that the thin metal of a car door would offer no protection.

The video also showed the effects on the human body of explosives. Bodies that had been too close to an exploding bomb or grenade looked like pieces of skinned meat. Some bodies looked peaceful, as if the person was sleeping; there were no visible injuries. The invisible killer had been the blast that had caused their lungs to explode and their bones to shatter.

Nigel stood in front of us and commented, 'It'll take more than an aspirin and a plaster to cure that lot. You are going to learn battlefield medical skills. By that I mean administering morphine, putting on field dressings and inserting drips.'

I looked around and saw that several of the lads had blanched; the very thought of needles made me swallow hard.

When Nigel called for a volunteer, Leanne stood up. From his bag Nigel produced a large needle and tube and told Leanne, 'Lie down. This won't hurt a bit.'

We laughed, but Leanne had gone white. He took a sterile pad and wiped it over the back of her hand and then, with one swift movement, pushed the needle into her vein. It was obvious that the needle had been correctly inserted as blood immediately began to flow into the tube. Nigel looked up and grinned. 'Easy isn't it, boys and girls? Guess what? Now it's your turn. Pick a partner and don't mess about; one day this could be for real.'

We were each issued with a candular needle and a rubber tourniquet. My partner was a tall, softly spoken Irishman called Dermot. He still had a black eye from the milling at Camp Alpha. Sportingly he offered me his hand. I did not have to use the tourniquet as the blue veins on the back stood out quite prominently. As I swabbed the area into which I was about to insert the needle, I glanced at Dermot's face. His eyes were tightly shut, his face was taut and he was breathing rapidly. Looking around I could see that he was not the only one to have this reaction. At the back of the hall Les was inserting a needle into Tony's hand. As he did so he passed out and fell to the floor with a dull thud. Tony's hand began to bleed.

I was amazed at how easy it was to insert a needle into a vein. Dermot winced as the needle hit home and his blood began to flow into the tube. Quickly I capped the end of the tube and told Dermot I had finished. He nodded, his eyes still tightly shut. Nigel came over to us and looked at my handiwork. 'Yeah, that's good.' he said, 'Take it out and swab.' I pulled the needle out and Dermot sighed with relief. Poor old Les was still out cold on the floor with Nigel shaking him and calling him a big girl's blouse.

Then it was Dermot's turn. He held my hand in a vicelike grip, the needle poised just above my vein. I decided to watch. At first I thought that Dermot was just going to plunge the needle in. Then he pulled back and the needle hovered over the back of my hand. Two or three times he came close to inserting the needle but each time he drew back as it touched my skin. 'I can't do it,' he whispered.

I began to feel uneasy. Nigel came over to see what was

happening. He took the needle from Dermot and slid it into my hand. I hardly felt a thing. Then he gave Dermot a clean needle and said, 'Right, it's your turn.'

Dermot gripped the needle again, took a deep breath and plunged the needle into my hand. I yelped with pain. The needle was certainly in my hand but it was nowhere near to a vein. Nigel took a look and told Dermot to try again. The next time he found the right spot but, as my blood began to flow, he suddenly gasped, 'I feel sick,' and rushed off towards the toilets. I sat there looking at Nigel, who merely shrugged his shoulders.

When everyone had inserted the needles successfully into their partner's hand Nigel told us we next had to do it to ourselves. One at a time we were given clean needles and told to get on with it. My hand was beginning to ache and I could see the start of a bruise, but I surprised myself by pushing the needle straight in. Some of the men were not able to inject themselves at all but the women managed it without too much fuss. Normally I hated needles but I realized that my life might depend upon my own quick actions one day. Seeing the way that some of the men reacted, convinced me I had to be able to rely on myself.

Eventually it was over but as we started to relax Nigel produced a half-inch needle, a small syrette and a bag of clear fluid. 'Morphine.' he said. 'If you get slotted, you'll need some of this.' As he spoke, he slammed his fist down hard on to Vince's thigh. Pulling his hand up again we could see that the syrette was now empty. Vince gripped his leg. 'Feeling dead, yet?' asked Nigel. Vince nodded, his face ashen. 'Well fortunately for you,' said Nigel, 'that was just because I thumped your leg. This is only water. Those of you that pass will be issued with a complete medical kit including morphine and drips.' He smiled and my heart sank as I realized what was coming next. 'Right,' he said, 'just before you go, each of you inject your leg.'

We queued to leave and Nigel handed us each a syringe. Gripping mine in my fist, I slammed my hand on to my leg. As I raised it again I was amazed to find that I had squeezed my hand on impact, pumping the contents directly into my leg. It was that easy to administer a shot of pain-relieving drugs. The next morning we compared bruises. My hand was black and blue and my leg was stiff, but at least I had done it.

Our time on the range was coming to an end. Bruce gave us some time to practise U and J turns in the range cars and that, at least, was great fun. It was also used to teach us the techniques of escaping from a difficult situation.

Two at a time we would hurtle along a lonely road, the wind whistling through the space where there had once been a windscreen. There were still shards of glass on the seats from the shattered windows and these dug into our backsides as we drove along. No one ever bothered to clean the insides of the cars. We practised U-turns by pulling on the handbrake, depressing the clutch and turning the steering wheel all at the same time. The two-litre cars slithered round, tyres squealing as the dust from the country road rose in clouds behind us. As the car came round a full 180 degrees, we took the handbrake off, slammed the car into gear and raced off in the direction from which we had just come. J turns were similar except they were performed in reverse gear.

The CQB ended and we sat around in the classroom cleaning our weapons and wondering what would happen next. The chief instructor looked at us and said, 'Don't become complacent. No one is even close to what is required of you yet. The next few weeks will sort out the men from the boys. You will be learning about all aspects of surveillance and it will be your bread and butter.'

Nina took over the briefing and told us that the surveillance phase would cover a number of subjects including close target recces or CTRs and the planning and setting up of observation posts. I had no idea what this would be about but I did know that those with infantry or marine backgrounds would be able to complete this phase standing on their heads. For the women it would be as new as the fieldcraft with which it went hand in hand.

CHAPTER NINE

We went back to the classroom the next day without having had any time off. Nina and Ken, the flat-nosed DS, took the theory lessons but explained that these would be followed by practical exercises out in the field.

We were given code sheets and told to learn the codes as homework; there would be no time to do it during the day. The codes were to be used when passing messages over the radio and, as they were not secure, it was essential that we become fluent with the terms we would have to use. *"Phonebook"* or *"dolphin"* meant return to base. *"Dish"* meant roundabout and *"fudge"* traffic lights. Target people were to be referred to as *"bulls eyes"* and target vehicles as *"goals"*. *"Tightrope"* meant that there was visual contact with the target and *"I see,"* meant that you had the target in sight and were able to give directions to the others. It was like learning a completely different language.

As I had suspected, some of the lads knew all about observation posts and they groaned when they heard they would have to sit through the lessons all over again.

Observation posts or OPs could be set up almost anywhere as long as there was sufficient cover. They were used to hide operators so that they could gather intelligence on terrorist activities. Sometimes OPs were set up in buildings, but often they were little more than bushes, ditches or rubbish tips. Depending on the type of operation to be carried out, they could be set up for as little as twenty-four hours or as much as two weeks. I was amazed at the amount of careful planning needed to set up a successful OP.

Once a target had been identified and the need for an OP had been established, the area had to be thoroughly checked. This was done, in the first instance, by the use of aerial photography and ordnance survey maps. Used together, they showed all the physical features of the area and helped us to identify the most suitable spot for an OP. Once the place had been chosen we had to find out other things about the area. For example, if we were to watch a house or other building we needed to know if there were any security lights or cameras in operation or whether there were dogs on the premises. Operators would be sent to the area to gather vital information and also get a feel for the place. This would help when considering possible areas for the drop-off and pick-up points for the operators and for re-supplying them. CTRs would be planned with the involvement of the whole team. They would be dropped off at a suitable point and would then scout the area, checking the route in and out across the fields. If possible they would also take photos of the neighbourhood. I began to see the importance of the training we had received in covert infra-red photography. If it were not possible to take photos, then sketch plans had to be drawn, with great attention being paid to the smallest details.Once all the preliminary work had been done, it was time for the team leader to plan his operation. Six pages of orders had to be completed. These included the names of both the operation itself and of the operators involved, the exact grid reference of where the OP was to be located and a short intelligence brief of the target. We had to have details of other security forces in the area and to know if there was a dedicated army unit on standby at a local barracks or police station.

Next the different phases of the operation itself had to be planned. The drop-off was the first thing to be considered and covered such things as the time of leaving the base, the number of cover cars and operators and the route to be taken. Details such as markers to the drop-off point or DOP were noted. These could be such things as a white gate, a telegraph pole or a gap in the hedge. Next came the walk in to the OP, the route being marked on the aerial photograph. The third phase covered both the construction of the OP and the routine to be adhered to once it had been set up. This phase also included timings for radio checks.

Phase five laid down procedures for the re-supplying of the OP and for the removal of rubbish and waste over the following days. Lastly, the drive back to base, the direction of travel and the cover had to be planned.

We also learned what to do if confronted by the enemy. It was really quite simple. If we were challenged with weapons we were told to shoot first before being shot ourselves. If they appeared to have no weapons there was the possibility of arresting them.

Because of the very real danger of a firefight, the quickest route to the nearest Accident and Emergency hospital was always to be pointed out. Since we would be in hostile territory it was not an option to wait for an ambulance in case of injury and so, should any of the operators be hurt, we were to drive them directly to the hospital. I could again appreciate the value of the medical training we had received.

The final part of the orders covered code words, meteorological information and synchronizing watches.

The theory kept us busy in the classroom for nearly a week. Every stage was covered in great detail. After all, our lives depended upon us understanding the orders and procedures.

When the practical side began Craig, the tall DS with permanent bags under his eyes, took the women out into the field. We were standing around in our camouflage gear amongst the gorse bushes when we suddenly heard a muffled voice say, 'Care to join me, ladies?' To my amazement Harry, streaked with green and brown camouflage paint, slithered out of a gorse bush. It was a small bush, quite low to the ground and covered in sharp thorns. Harry explained how this and other similar bushes could be turned into very effective OPs.

He pointed out that to remain undiscovered you had to be very careful how you got into the bush in the first place. After a couple of days any broken branches would be dead and would show up against the live vegetation. It was important that the area around the entrance should remain undisturbed. Army boots would churn up grass and mud so a ground sheet was put down at the entrance point. We also learned to tie back branches so that someone crawling into the middle of the bush would not damage them. Once he was safely inside he could cut the string and allow the branches to fall back into their natural position. Further cover could be provided by the use of camouflage netting inside the bush. Conditions were very cramped. There was usually only enough space for two men to lie side by side. All the provisions and spare equipment had to be kept in a rucksack or bergen, and food had to be wrapped in cling film so that the smell would not attract vermin or dogs. Calls of nature were taken either in bottles or plastic bags.

During the height of summer the heat could be stifling and insect bites caused a lot of irritation. Winter was no better and the cold and rain could easily force a team out before frostbite set in.

After we had listened to what Harry had to say we practised making our own OPs. Julia and I teamed up and spent ages making sure that we did not do too much damage to the bush we had chosen. Once inside I lay down watching the target area with Julia at my back guarding the rear with her pistol. Craig strolled over and looked long and hard at the bush. I tried to hold my breath; we both kept perfectly still as he bent down and peered through the leaves. Then he stood up and said, 'Not bad, ladies. But your Parker pen has given you away, Jules.'

We crawled out and Julia blushed as she checked her pockets only to discover that her pen was indeed missing. It was a very simple error but one which could easily have compromised our position had it occurred over the water. At the very worst it could have cost us our lives.

It had been a long day and we went back to the training school where Craig took us into a classroom. He explained to us that it was not the role of women to insert OPs. We would be used solely as pick-up and drop-off drivers. Sensing that Julia was about to interrupt him, Craig said, 'Jules, you know as well as I do, women are non-combat. It's the rules . . .' Julia, her face red with anger exploded, 'That's bollocks!'

Leanne began to laugh. It was the first time that any of us had heard Julia use any word that even resembled a profanity. Craig tried again, 'I don't make the rules. If it were up to me I would let you go out and freeze your arse off. It would save me doing it. But that's the way it is.' He escaped before Julia could say any more. She was still furious and as we sat there waiting for our next instructions she said, 'This is crap. We've been through all this just so that we can become glorified taxi drivers.'

At that moment Nina walked in and sat down with us. 'I hear that you've been giving Craig a hard time,' she said. Then she patiently explained that for some of the operations women were just not allowed on the ground. It really did not make sense to any of us. We were being trained by the soldiers from some of the most elite regiments in the world. We were doing everything the men did and we had proved ourselves to be just as good as they were and yet, when it came to front-line service, the Army had decided that we were not good enough. The official view was archaic and patronizing. Apparently the main objections to women manning OPs were that it would be difficult for a woman to urinate in such conditions and what would we do if one of us had a period? Obviously the world would grind to a halt! It seemed that we women would never win.

Nina tried to lift our spirits by telling us that once the surveillance phase started, we would see what our value would be. We would be doing things the men could only dream of. We trundled out and went to Leanne's room for a cup of coffee. There we sat and discussed the attitude of the Army towards women. To us it seemed about as up to date as the dinosaurs and we all looked forward to the day when it would wake up to itself and see that we were just as capable as the men.

The following day Ken told us that the practical side of the course was about to begin. We were split into teams, mine consisting of Rory, Chris and Harry, the DS. The object of the exercise was to insert an OP into a farm that was suspected of being used by IRA members. The day began. I drove along the narrow country lanes towards the target in the Opel Ascona; Chris was beside me, navigating. We could see the target building to our left, surrounded by woodland. Chris noticed a white gate and muttered something about a possible drop-off. We went back to camp and sat poring over the maps, trying to decide on the best drive in. Orders were prepared for a CTR that night.

At midnight we drove silently out of camp. Harry had gone ahead so that he would be there to shadow the team. Chris and Rory were wearing their combats and, as we drove, they began to apply camouflage paint. They were carrying a bergen containing a camera and a radio. It was very dark and we struggled to find the drop-off markers.

Suddenly out of nowhere the white gate appeared and I jammed on the brakes, stopping in a shower of gravel about ten yards beyond it. Rory and Chris jumped out of the car, slamming the doors behind them. I drove slowly away, listening all the time for their radio check. Then I pulled into a lay-by about a mile or so away and waited for them. I had to wait for a couple of hours and spent the time studying the map, trying to memorize the route back in. Then came the call to pick them up. I drove back along unfamiliar roads, not very confident that I would find them. They had obviously seen me because over the radio came the call, 'Three Zero, you've missed us!'

I had to drive on for a further half a mile before I could find a place to turn around; then I drove back towards them, nervous in case I missed them for a second time. They were watching for me and Chris poked his head out and began waving. I stopped the car and they got in. This time Harry was with them. He said that we would de-brief on the way back and told me to turn round at the next left turn.

I found the turning. It was the entrance to a farm and was on an incline. As I swung round in the entrance I put my foot down but, to my horror, the car began rolling backwards. I floored the accelerator and the engine screamed but still we rolled backwards. Then, from the back, I heard Harry shout, 'Into gear!' and as I crunched my way to the right gear we shot off into the darkness, tyres spinning. In the rear view mirror I could see Harry shaking his head. 'Not very covert, was it?' he enquired mildly.

As we drove back towards camp Harry explained that we had made some very common mistakes. The markers to a drop-off had to be visible at night as well as during the day, enabling the driver to see the drop-off and glide to a stop, rather than slam on the brakes and screech to a halt, as I had done. Rory and Chris had slammed the car doors as they got out, rather than pushing them silently shut. Harry also told me that I should have been constantly relaying my position to them while driving to the pick up. It was not done to jump out and wave like Chris had done, as he could not have been sure that it was my headlights he had seen.

It was obvious that we still had a lot of practising to do and we spent the next few nights doing nothing else. Then the day dawned when we had to insert an OP for real. I was teamed up with Glen and Guy this time and felt much more confident than I had the first time.

I drove them to the drop off and glided silently to a stop. They got out and disappeared into the darkness. They had selected a ditch covered by hedgerow for their OP. It gave them a good view of their target, a farm building across a field. Having dropped them I drove off and heard their reassuring radio check then parked and waited for the call to tell me that they were in the OP. It came just before five am when Glen shouted that the OP was in and functional. I drove back to camp to snatch a couple of hours of sleep before I had to plan their re-supply.

Back at camp Julian and Rob were manning the communications room. This was in preparation for their duties over the water. They were officers, and officers invariably became Detachment Commanders, Intelligence Liaison officers or operational planners.

At around midday I was in the canteen sorting out re-supply rations when Craig burst in. He pointed at me and shouted, 'You. Out here now!'

I ran outside to see cars driven by DS speeding out of the camp. I followed Craig into the comms room. Julian sat hunched over a map. He was talking to Glen on the radio. Craig said, 'Tell them to stay calm. We are on the way.'

He turned to me, a smile on his face and said, 'The bloody hunt found them!'

It seemed that Guy and Glen had been sitting quite happily in their OP when hounds, frantically baying and snapping, suddenly surrounded them. The huntsmen, hearing the noise and seeing the hounds pawing the ground, had dismounted and gone to investigate. When they found two armed young men, dressed in army combats, they became very suspicious and called the police. The DS arrived at the scene after the police and amid all the ensuing chaos managed to give a code word to the police which, when checked, verified that they were in fact soldiers. The police backed off and the intrepid pair were bundled into a car and driven back to camp to be given the biggest bollocking of their lives. Then they were fined a tenner each. We had a lot to learn from their misfortune. In a live situation they could have been shot or captured. At the very least their position would have been compromised and the terrorist alerted to the interest being shown in him.

The exercises continued, night after night. I was dog-tired. After the OP had been inserted I had a long drive back to camp and only managed to get two or three hours' sleep before breakfast. Then it was off to the comms room for an update, followed by the planning of a re-supply. Once that had been done we took turns in the comms room, ensuring that every team on the ground was radio checked. Finally the OPs were all extracted and Craig told us that the following day we would have a map-reading exercise.

CHAPTER TEN

Early the next morning, a Saturday, we assembled in camouflage kit and after breakfast Norman, the senior DS, briefed us. We were to travel light, in pairs, with only a bottle of water each and a pack of rations. These consisted of a couple of sandwiches and a Mars bar. We also had maps and compasses, which we had to carry ourselves, as we were not allowed to take bergens. I was paired with Mike and we were told that we would be dropped off and would have to navigate a fifteen-mile course over difficult terrain.

We travelled in silence. As we got close to our destination it began to get dark and when we were dropped off it started to rain. We were not wearing waterproofs and soon our combat jackets were soaked through. We began to climb almost immediately; the mountainside was the steepest I had ever encountered. Almost immediately we were shrouded in mist and low cloud. Mike had the compass and we slowly followed the bearing, unable to see any of the reference points. We plodded along in our wet clothes. We were freezing cold by now and it was more by luck than judgement that we stumbled upon the first checkpoint. We found two SAS men wrapped in waterproofs, huddled around the stove in a tent and drinking steaming hot mugs of tea. They took our names, then pointed us in the direction of the next checkpoint and told us to bugger off.

We descended quickly, tumbling on the rough ground. The next leg took us across the valley and back up the other side. It was still raining and my wet clothing chafed against my legs. Mike and I had decided to run to keep warm but this soon stopped when we reached the next steep incline. We climbed back up into the clouds. We were freezing; even breathing was painful. Mike's whole body was beginning to shake. We reached the next checkpoint; this too was manned by individuals who could not care less about us. They were probably annoyed at having to give up a Saturday for this exercise.

We carried on, plodding along in single file. It was still raining hard and was getting colder. Mike stopped and as I came up to him I could see that he was in trouble. His face was deathly pale and he was whispering, 'I can't go on.'

I took hold of his arm and we began the slow descent into the valley again. His co-ordination had gone and he could hardly stand. Holding on to each other we tumbled down the side of the mountain. Eventually the cloud broke and I could see the valley below. My knees were aching with the strain of the descent and of trying to keep Mike upright. Our map was so wet and torn that it was no longer of any use to us. Once we were down in the valley we staggered along the footpath like two drunks. The wind was blowing the rain almost horizontally at us and it was unbelievably cold. Mike had his arm around my shoulder. I kept talking to him and trying to get him to talk to me but he was rambling incoherently. I was desperate to find shelter and to get help for him.

In the distance I could just make out the shape of a low brick building at the side of a lake. Parked alongside the building was the unmistakable shape of a Land Rover. Mike's legs buckled and I shouted at him to stand up and keep going. My hands were so cold and numb that I could no longer keep hold of his jacket. Then I saw the Land Rover bumping its way towards us and realized that we had been spotted. Soon we had been bundled into the back and wrapped in blankets. Our saviour was the ever-faithful medic, Nigel, who attended to Mike while his mate drove the Land Rover at breakneck speed.

Nigel was mumbling, 'Bloody idiots,' and told me that he had warned the DS that this was a foolhardy exercise and that we were not properly equipped for the task in hand. Another team was missing and Julia had succumbed to hypothermia. Mike was taken to hospital while the rest of us were driven back to camp with instructions to take hot baths and to rest.

Later that evening we were told to assemble in the lecture hall. In walked Norman, his face as fierce as ever. Then, to our utter amazement, he gave us all a bollocking for putting our lives at risk. I could hardly believe what I was hearing. This was the man who had sent us up the mountain in the first place and now he was blaming us for having obeyed his instructions. We were all stunned and sat there listening to his harsh northern accent in complete silence. When he finished he walked towards the door and, as he reached it, a voice from the back of the hall bellowed, 'Fucking wanker!' Norman paused and then walked out, closing the door behind him. The mood in the room was mutinous. Many of us were on the point of giving up. We may all have been volunteers, but to be treated like this was too much. Not surprisingly, the DS kept well away from us for the remainder of that night.

The next day was quiet. We were told that it was to be an easy day and that we would not have to assemble in the lecture hall until seven pm. Although the day was officially designated as 'easy' we had washing and ironing to catch up on and the time passed very quickly. Seven pm arrived and we gathered in the lecture room. In walked Norman accompanied by several other DS. The sight of Norman made me feel very ill at ease.

We were split into teams of three, with a DS allocated to each team, and were told to go to the motor pool. John was waiting for us and soon a long line of cars followed him out into the road. We had been driving for about ten minutes when the radio burst into life. The message was, 'Two Nine, Three Zero, Three One and Three Two, phonebook.'

The four cars with these numbers slowed down, then turned and headed back towards the camp. The rest of us continued down the road behind John. Twenty minutes later we pulled into a pub car park. John jumped out of his car and beckoned to the rest of us to follow him. Inside the pub we found more students accompanied by DS. Not wanting to break the habits of a lifetime, John sat down and ordered Vince to buy a round.

I wondered what this was all leading to, but when I asked Ben he only shrugged his shoulders. John broke the silence by telling us that those who had been called back to camp had been 'binned' and that the rest of us had made it through to the next stage. He continued, 'When you get back to camp do not engage the others in conversation. Anyone who does will be joining them on the first bus out tomorrow. Understood?' Julia asked the obvious question. 'Why have they gone?' John looked around at us all and said, 'Because they are crap; not up to it. Need I say more?'

We all fell silent; twelve students had gone in one fell swoop. All the women were still there, but Mike was missing, so were Glen and Guy. Jack had also gone; he was a cocky little sod and I would not miss him at all. I had plenty of sympathy for the others though. It was an awful way to get rid of them, especially after all the effort they had put into the training. I just hoped that the news was given to them in a more civilized manner. Although we now knew that those of us still sitting in the pub were safe for the moment, our spirits were low. It had been an awful weekend and it did not seem right to be sitting drinking pints when back at camp twelve of our friends were packing up, ready to go home.

The next morning after breakfast Ted told us to get into our tracksuits and we were taken to one of the low brick buildings close to the range. It was cold and gloomy inside and we huddled together for warmth. In the centre was a huge square made of gym mats. As we sat there shivering a huge, muscle-bound SAS man, wearing only a thin singlet and baggy tracksuit bottoms, walked in. He strutted past us, the look on his face one of utter contempt. He raised one arm and, pointing at Julian grunted, 'You. Unarmed combat.' He grabbed Julian and in a flash had sent him sprawling across the mat, face down and with his arm pulled at a ninety-degree angle behind his back. Julian groaned in agony and, as the SAS man tweaked his wrist, he screamed.

Releasing his hold he stepped over Julian and pointed to me. 'Your turn,' he said. I stepped forward and he grabbed me, spinning me round to face the group, as he announced, 'First technique . . . goose neck.' I felt him pull my arm behind me and ram it up my back. My wrist, which was caught in a vicelike grip, felt as if it were on fire. Every so often he would apply pressure to the wrist, bending it and causing pains to shoot up my arm. There was no way I could escape. Eventually he let go of my arm and I nursed my wrist, which was by now completely numb.

We split into pairs and practised simple methods of restraint with arms pulled behind backs. When he was satisfied that he had inflicted sufficient pain, Muscleman called us to one side and dropped down onto the bare concrete where he performed twenty press-ups. Then, balancing on one hand, he did twenty more. The man was obviously some kind of sadist and we all knew what would happen next. We started a series of press-ups, bare knuckles against the concrete floor. I was in agony after completing only five. Then he made us practise forward and backward rolls. I could not see any point to this but later on in the course it became clear why this training was necessary.

By lunchtime we were bruised and aching. We sat in the sun outside the building, gratefully eating the stew they had brought out for us. Muscleman came over and looked at us lounging around. 'Right,' he shouted, 'Now I'm going to show you how to disable an attacker without resorting to weapons.'

He dragged Ben to his feet and showed us how to cause the maximum amount of discomfort to a person by jabbing fingers into their eyes. I winced as Ben doubled over, hands covering his face. Muscleman continued, 'Next, fingers up the nose.' He advanced towards Rob but by now everyone had the same idea and we scattered in all directions.

'OK,' he said, 'no more demos.' He had obviously had his fun for the day and began talking to us in a more civilized manner.

He told us that if we were ever in a tight situation and unable to use our weapons, our lives might depend on unarmed combat. Fighting dirty might be the only way out, especially for the women who were not as strong as the men. Ramming your fingers into someone's eyes or up their noses and scratching or biting were all acceptable techniques. However, like everything else we had learned, it had to be an automatic reaction; there would be no time to be squeamish. Luckily these were not the kind of skills that could be practised on each other. Ben's eyes

1. An explosive device is activated during car drill at Camp Alpha. The activation of the device is the signal for the operators to start firing at the targets through the windscreen.

2. Jackie practises firing from a moving from a car with another female operator behind the wheel.

3. More car drill. This time the puffs of smoke above the vehicle are from live rounds being fired over the operators' heads to give them a sense of being shot at.

4. Jackie in the prone position laying down aimed shots as covering fire during car drill. On this occasion she is using a 9mm Browning pistol.

5. Two car drill at Camp Alpha. The cars used during training were those which had previously been compromised in Northern Ireland.

6. Jackie allows another operator to escape from the car by laying down covering fire using a Heckler and Koch MP5K 9mm submachine gun. The MP5K is the weapon favoured by security and special forces.

7. Jackie and another operator prepare to do a room assault using stun grenades.

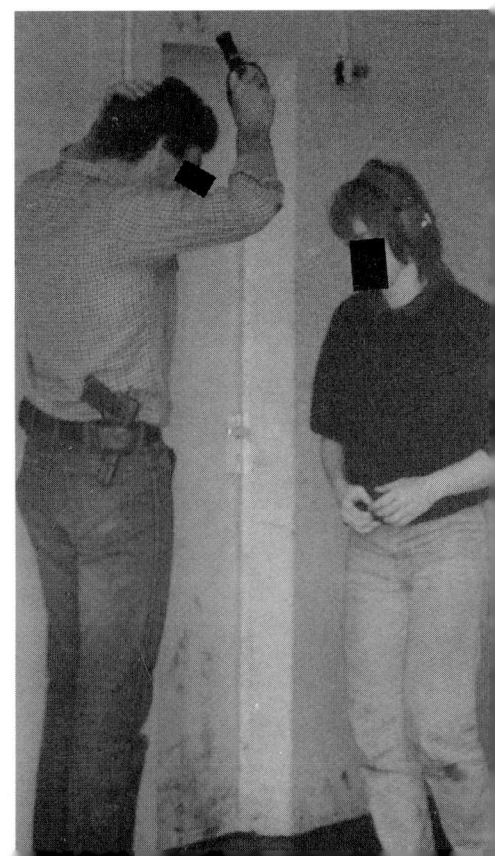

8. Wrong! Neither Jackie nor her companion have the potential 'target' covered at this stage.

9. The other operator exits from cover with his MP5K. Note his secondary weapon the Browning pistol he carries in his waist band.

10. An SAS Instructor briefs Jackie and other operators before a house assault.

11. Jackie photographed from a covert camera during operations in Northern Ireland as she walks away from a target. Jackie's hand in her pocket, tightly gripping a Walther PPK.

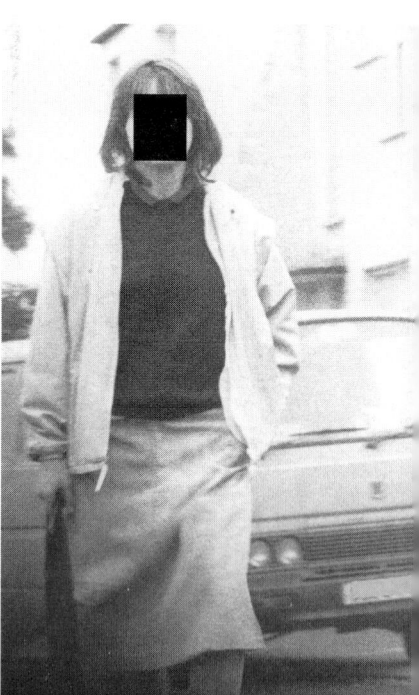

were still streaming and I am sure that, had Muscleman done this in a live situation, he would have been blinded.

The day ended with a jog back to camp. That night Liz shocked us all by telling us that she was leaving. I was sad to see her go but she said that the course was just not for her. That left just eighteen of us, four of whom were women.

For the next two weeks we continued with our weapon training. We learned about the MP5K, a short, stocky machine pistol favoured by the SAS and used to great effect during the Iranian embassy siege. It was a strange-looking weapon that could fire either single or multiple bursts.

On the first day Brian and Bruce showed us how to strip the weapon, how it worked and all the important safety drills. We were told that over the water we would be carrying an MP5K along with another rifle in our vehicles and that we would have a pistol in our belts. We practised double tapping with the MP5K on the ranges. It was deadly accurate and we were surprised by the lack of recoil.

The most important thing now was to practise car drills. At first we were in pairs, the passenger using the MP5K to lay down initial fire, with the driver relying on his pistol. In a real contact situation the driver would not have time to reach behind him for his other weapon. Then the fun began when we practised in fours, with three of us using MP5Ks. In the heat of the moment it was easy to slip the catch from single to multiple shot and empty a thirty-round magazine within two seconds. Care also had to be taken as we ran back towards our cars, crossing each other's line of fire.

By the time we finished we were breathing hard. Our levels of concentration were enormous, as it was imperative that we shouted instructions controlling the movements of the others. The noise of the rounds being put down was reduced to a dull roar by our ear defenders and, to complicate things even more, Brian simulated an op down, shot and slumped in his vehicle. This was a situation that had happened before over the water and would, no doubt, happen again. It was a difficult situation to simulate on a range using paper targets. After we had tried a few times, Brian collected us together and said, 'Right ho, let's try this down on the farm.' This was fairly close to the range and consisted of a number of farm buildings and sheds. It was used to demonstrate the technique of containing an area.

Brian told Ben to drive in to the farm and the two cover cars then had to react to whatever happened. Ben drove off, his car exhaust blowing. I sat next to Vince and behind me were Leanne and Jamie. Mark and Carl were in the second car. Ben was already out of sight. From the direction of the farm came the sound of gunfire and we heard Ben shouting over the radio, *'Contact, contact!'* This was the phrase that was used only if an op had been seriously compromised or was about to get into a firefight.

Vince gunned the engine of our car and we sped off in a cloud of dust. The farm came into view and we skidded into the courtyard. Ahead of us we could see Ben's car. The door was open and he was slumped, half in and half out of it. Vince made a perfect handbrake turn, as did Mark behind us. I leapt out of the car and sprinted for the cover of a low brick wall. Leanne and Jamie ran over to Ben. It was strange to be outside the confines of the range with no visible targets. Leanne covered Jamie as he dragged Ben from the car. Carl and Mark were also out of their car and were covering too. Suddenly one of the admin staff walked into view. 'You Brit bastards,' she shouted, picked up a stone and threw it at Leanne. It missed her and bounced off the car.

From nowhere ten of the admin staff appeared all dressed in civvies and all shouting and throwing stones at us. I stood up and aimed my weapon at the group, shouting, 'Stand back. Security force.' I was not sure what I thought I would achieve by this. All I got in response was a hail of stones and someone shouting, 'Fuck off, you Brit bastard.'

A shot rang out and from the direction of the barn came more firing. The crowd cheered and we returned fire. Ben was, by now, in my car and Jamie was shouting for us to retreat. I sprinted across the open courtyard and dived into the car. Then, with wheels spinning, we sped out of the yard.

When we arrived back at the range we debriefed. The DS had been watching the entire scene and were pleased that we had decided not to fire into the crowd of unarmed civilians. They then briefed us on the next test, in which we had to walk into the farm courtyard individually and deal with whatever might happen while we were there. One by one the students disappeared from the range. Soon I was the only one left. Brian drove me down to the farm and told me that the only thing I needed to know was that the car I would find in the yard was mine. Then he gave me the keys and dropped me off.

As I walked towards the courtyard I was glad that I had my pistol tucked into my waistband. I turned into the yard and saw nothing. Coming round a corner, I encountered two men who stepped in front of me. One was Ken, the other was a blond SAS man who had the appearance of a fierce Viking warrior. I could also see the butt of a pistol tucked into his belt. I looked away, not wanting to make eye contact. Then I heard Ken's familiar voice, asking me where I was going. I stopped and pointed lamely towards the car. Ken asked if it was my car and when I said that it was he told me that he wanted it. I began to back away, all the while desperately trying to think what to do. The Viking grunted, 'She's a Brit,' and as he spoke I swung back my jacket and pulled out my pistol. It was too late. Ken, realizing that this is what I would do, had grabbed me in a bear hug. I could not move. I had no chance to poke his eyes or stick my fingers up his nose. The only thing I managed to do was to side-swipe him with my head. The resulting clash of our heads obvious hurt me more than it did him. Then his mate picked me up by the arm and swung me into the side of a farm building.

The next thing that I remember was lying, face down, on the ground with both my arms shoved behind my back. I could taste blood in my mouth and felt a warm trickle coming from my nose. My head was thumping and all I could think of was, 'Jesus, I want my mother.' Then a shot rang out and Ken hauled me to my feet, telling me, 'You've just been executed. Shot dead by your own weapon.' I wiped my nose on my sleeve and walked around the corner. When I was well out of sight, I burst into tears of frustration. The stupidity of having been caught out in this way was just too much for me.

Bruce came after me and asked if I was OK. He produced a grimy tissue and wiped my face. Then he patiently explained what I had done wrong. He told me that I should have thrown the car keys at the gruesome twosome, let them walk to the car and then have shot them.

He began to chuckle. 'If it makes you feel any better,' he said, 'everyone so far had ended up eating dirt. You should see poor old Julian . . .' Julian, being an officer, came in for a lot of stick. He had ended up in a fistfight and had come off worst, with his nose flattened across his face. He had then been kicked a few times for good measure.

Brian then announced that we would be going to the 'Killing House' and early the next morning we arrived at the SAS barracks in Camp Alpha.

The 'Killing House' was a purpose-built house and was used by the regiment to perfect the technique of rapid entry into rooms. The main room was furnished but the sofa was full of bullet holes and the stuffing was falling out. There was a gallery, protected by bullet-proof glass, from where everything that happened in the room could be observed. The glass was pitted where the bullets had hit and I was not sure that I would have wanted to stand behind it. We, of course, were not given a choice. Leanne was selected as a 'volunteer' and told to sit on the sofa. The rest of us were herded up to the gallery to watch what was about to happen.

The room was dimly lit and Leanne sat on the sofa waiting, her body rigid. Then the door burst open and dark figures rushed in to the sounds of gunfire and exploding thunderflashes. One of the dark figures grabbed Leanne and pulled her out of the room. There were one or two more bursts of gunfire and then everything went quiet. The demonstration was over.

We left the gallery and went back down the stairs. Leanne was nowhere to be seen; she had fled to the nearest toilet, which was not surprising when one considered what she had just been through. The dark figures filed back into the room and lined up in front of our group, MP5Ks slung casually across their chests. They all wore black overalls and hoods and their faces were obscured by black gasmasks. It was a sinister sight. When they pulled off the masks we were confronted with the smiling faces of Brian, Bruce, Will and Jez. 'Easy, isn't it, mates?' one of them enquired.

Of course it was not easy, as we discovered when we began to practise the drill ourselves. We had been divided into groups of four and, each time we entered, the room had been arranged in a different way. The lighting was always kept quite low and there were a number of targets to represent both terrorists and innocent civilians or hostages.

On a given signal, Number One had to kick down the door. Number Two then rushed into the room, followed by Number One, and fired at the terrorist targets. Numbers Three and Four entered and, in pairs, we began to clear the room, checking wardrobes, overturning beds, engaging the targets with well-aimed shots.

The next day we practised the drill again, this time wearing the dark overalls and hoods and the rubber respirators. The close-fitting hoods made it hard to hear properly and the gasmasks made breathing difficult. With every breath came the horrible smell of rubber and the plastic eyepieces of the masks restricted our vision.

For this exercise I was Number Two with Ben at Number One, ready to break down the door. Behind me at Number Three stood Vince, with his hand on my shoulder and behind him Liam, at Number Four. The adrenalin began to flow. I held up my arm and began the count down. Three – two – one. As I reached one, Ben kicked in the door and I rushed into the room to the left, followed by Ben, who veered to the right. In front of me was a paper target. I double tapped and pushed past it, looking round as I did so. Jamie was sitting on the sofa, beside a terrorist target. I shot at the target and watched as paper and wood flew into the air. Ben grabbed Jamie by the scruff of his neck and Vince shouted to indicate that the room was clear. We backed out and, once we were clear of the room, pulled off the gas masks, our faces flushed and sweaty. Liam grinned at Jamie and said, 'I didn't expect to see you in there, Shorty!', to which Jamie replied, 'I'm just glad that you mad bastards didn't shoot me.' We all knew that we were playing for real now. One false move and a colleague could be dead.

Brian seemed pleased with our progress and told us that since the weekend was approaching we could all have some time off. He insisted that we leave the camp but said that we must return by Sunday evening. We discovered that this gesture was not as generous as it had at first seemed. There was to be a reunion at the camp that weekend and all the students had to leave to make room for the ex-operators who would be staying for a drunken party.

Leanne and I decided to let our hair down and found a cheap B & B in Bristol. There we had a relaxing time shopping and moaning about the DS, which made us feel better. Then, after a decent meal, we got drunk. Sunday went by in a flash and we soon found ourselves back in camp, where we discovered we were to meet up in the bar.

Harry, Alistair and Craig were waiting for us there and told us that the next phase of our training would start the following day and that it would be the most telling of all – surveillance. So that was it; the phase that would make or break us.

CHAPTER ELEVEN

Stuart and Nina conducted the initial lessons in surveillance techniques. They drummed it into us that we had to blend into the background wherever we happened to be. We were to become "grey men and women". They then issued us with books of maps that covered the area around the training camp.

Each major town or large village was colour-coded. The main street was shown as brown, as were A roads. B roads were blue and minor roads yellow. Motorways were coloured green. Each junction had a coloured spot with a number written on it. We used these colour codes to pass on information.

Foot surveillance was the next subject on the agenda. We had to know how to conceal a radio in our clothes, in the back of jeans or strapped to an arm. The operating wires had to be threaded down a sleeve or into a pocket and we wore tiny earpieces so that we could receive messages. It was imperative that we wore loose clothing, as we not only had to hide the radios, we also had pistols and magazines to conceal.

Our first practical exercises took us to two small towns. There we followed the DS who were forever changing direction, trying to lose us in the crowded shops. This part of the training was easier for the women than the men. No one gave a second glance to a woman wandering aimlessly around the shops. We blended in well with the genuine shoppers. The men fared less well as they looked awkward and out of place. The most difficult thing we had to learn was how to send messages while following a target. Often the communications were bad and the radio reception was distorted. This made it difficult for the person on the receiving end, as they had no idea of the location of the target. For the person passing the message it was equally frustrating, as by the time they had been asked to repeat what they had said the target had often moved on. There was also a tendency while repeating a message to speak louder than before. We must have looked really peculiar talking loudly into our armpits or shoulders where our microphones had been hidden.

Our next task was to learn the art of mobile surveillance. For this to work, teams of four or five cars were used. Eventually, when we had more experience, we would use two cars, one with a single occupant and the other with two people for support. Then we would each have a personal radio in case we needed to leave our vehicles to go *"foxtrot"*.

For the purpose of this exercise we were briefed on the identity of the target and the make of their vehicle, and we were told where we should position ourselves to begin the surveillance.

Two students were left back at base to man the communications room. The rest of us piled into two cars and drove off to stake out a town or village. After a while someone would shout over the radio, *"Stand by, stand by, Three Nine has Goal One at the dish towards the brown."* This roughly meant that, "Call sign Three Nine had visual contact with the target vehicle at the roundabout towards the main street." This was our signal to begin following the car.

In order not to be seen we would change places, every so often overtaking each other so that it did not appear as if we were driving along in a procession. Sometimes we used parallel routes, dodging in and out of the traffic but with one of us always trying to keep the target in sight. The person designated as navigator kept a close check on the radio messages being sent by the car that had visual contact with the target. The target car itself was driven by a DS and simulated the actions taken by terrorists in Northern Ireland. They frequently changed directions and carried out anti-surveillance, sometimes driving two or three times round a roundabout or into a cul de sac. We had to learn how to pull back without being seen and how to stay close but not so close that it was obvious what we were doing. We also had to judge each situation so that if they began anti-surveillance we could pull away completely. We frequently lost the target. When this happened the team would split up, with each of the cars taking a different route in the hope of spotting the target vehicle again. If either of us managed to re-establish contact, the car which had the target in its sight would relay a message to the others and the frantic game of "catch up" would begin. It was during situations such as these that I appreciated the advanced driving course we had taken.

One day in late November we were on a routine exercise along country lanes. Kate was driving the lead car and, with Liam and Rob, was following the target. I was with Julian in the car behind. Kate indicated that at the next junction she wanted to pull over and I acknowledged her message and told her that we would assume the lead. I told Julian to get ready to overtake. Before we reached the junction a red Opel overtook us and cut in behind Kate's car. It began to slow down until, just before we reached the junction, it was travelling at almost walking pace. I knew that there was no chance that we could take the lead as planned and so passed that message to Kate. By now Ben's car which was following us had caught up and Vince, the passenger, was looking impatient. Suddenly the radio crackled into life and I could hear Kate's voice shouting, 'Contact, contact.' Then there was silence.

Julian revved the engine and swung out onto the verge to pass the Opel. It pulled over slightly and as we passed it I could see that the driver was Stuart, one of the DS. Ben, sticking close to our rear bumper, overtook as well. We raced along the narrow lane until, skidding round a bend, we came across Kate's car. The doors were open and the car was empty. Julian shot past, narrowly missing the car and we screeched to a halt right across the junction, a minor crossroad.

We leapt out of our car, leaving it blocking the road. Our pistols were drawn as we dived for cover. Three other cars had also stopped and there were twelve students milling about, all brandishing pistols and waiting for something to happen.

There was no sign of Kate, Liam or Rob, but we could hear an engine as a car approached. A rusty old Fiesta, driven by a young lad, came around the bend. The passenger was another young boy. Seeing that the road was blocked they stopped, to be confronted by a number of students all aiming guns at them. One of the students shouted, 'You, in the car . . . OUT!' and the two boys tumbled out of the Fiesta, hands in the air and looking panic-stricken. 'Don't shoot,' one of them whimpered.

Stuart had by now caught us up and had parked the Opel behind us. He ran past me, pushing Ben and Vince aside, and yelled, 'Put those fucking pistols down, you idiots.' His face was red and it was obvious that he was furious with us. It was our turn to back off.

Then Nina appeared from the other direction, accompanied by Kate, Liam and Rob. She and Stuart spent a considerable amount of time apologizing to the two young lads and thanking them for participating in an army exercise. It was probably the most exciting thing that had ever happened to them, but one that they would not want to repeat. We had learned a valuable lesson. In Ireland our actions may well have been appropriate, but pointing firearms at innocent people going about their business in the countryside around our training camp was another matter altogether.

December came and we moved down south to learn the technique of surveillance in a big city.

At night we sat around, studying our maps and trying to memorize all the coloured spots. Then we spent three days driving around the entire area, trying to orientate ourselves. One place in particular was difficult to work as there had recently been riots there with fighting between the locals and the police. If we had made any cock-ups there, we might have been mistaken for undercover police and started the rioting again.

Our first job involved Mark and me acting as a newly married couple. We booked into a B & B and used our bedroom as an observation post to watch another B & B across the street, where there were DS holed up. I packed my bag with radio equipment, cameras, logs, an MP5K, a toothbrush and a change of underwear. The bedroom was dingy, but, having set up our radios and put the cameras on their tripods, we sat back to admire the view. Our colleagues were in vehicles parked in the area, waiting for us to report any movements from the B & B. Mark and I decided to split the work and have two hours on followed by two hours off. The time dragged; nothing happened and every hour we reported, 'No change.'

The street below us only came to life during the night when the dim lights attracted the girls. They would wander up and down as cars cruised by, occasionally stopping for the driver to have a brief conversation with a girl before opening the car door to let her in. In less than an hour she would be back on the street, looking for the next customer. It was during one of these scenes that Harry suddenly emerged from the B & B and walked towards a car that had slowed down and had its passenger door open. Before Harry could reach the car one of the girls had gone over to it and was trying to get in. There was a heated exchange as he manhandled her out of the way. The situation was resolved and within thirty seconds the street was back to normal. Mark had captured everything on film but we had had to wait for twelve hours for that small scene.

We stayed in that dismal room for two days, the Do Not Disturb sign firmly fixed to the door. Occasionally one of us would venture out, having called up one of the team to fetch us a take away and a fresh flask of coffee. It was not possible for us both to leave at the same time. To do so would have meant we would have had to pack up all our gear and take it with us, which might have aroused some suspicion amongst the staff on the reception desk.

Hour after hour we gazed out of the window, boredom and lack of sleep making it hard to concentrate. The only relief we had was a radio that we tuned to Radio One. My overwhelming memory of those few days was the sound of the Kajagoogoo hit, "Too Shy" being played incessantly. Harry hardly moved at all. He went out only twice and the team lost him once. We could hear the tension in their voices over the radio as they drove round and round the city trying to locate him. Eventually we got the call to return to base.

Mark and I packed up all our gear and went downstairs to pay the bill.

'Good weekend, Sir?' the slimy receptionist enquired of Mark. 'See you again, Mr Jones,' he said as he counted out our change. 'I doubt it very much,' Mark muttered in reply.

We walked around the corner and were picked up by Rod who immediately began complaining, 'You've had it easy for two days, shagging in a hotel while we froze our bollocks off.' That set the tone for what was to follow. It was typical of squaddie mentality to assume that if a man and a woman spent any time alone together they must have been at it like rabbits.

It was getting very close to Christmas and the city was packed. Foot surveillance became a nightmare. You only had to lose concentration for a second and the target was gone. No one liked to lose a target, but we all did it from time to time and gave ourselves a mental kick for being such idiots.

We moved to a disused Territorial Army camp outside town. The wooden huts reminded me of Camp Alpha. We set up a comms room and worked out a roster for manning it. The team was now split and the daunting prospect of working alone loomed large upon the horizon. John briefed us and told Jamie and Rod that they had to set up an observation post on some waste ground to watch a suspected terrorist hide. The rest of us would rotate in teams of four over a 24-hour period. I was on the first team out and drove out of camp alone, checking that I had my map book, pencil, torch and notebook on the passenger seat by my side. On the back seat was a bag containing my sub-machine gun.

I found a side street and parked. The OP team had already been dropped and I knew I had a long night ahead of me. I slouched in my seat, shivering with the cold. The cars parked around me were glistening with a covering of frost and the street was deathly quiet. By four am the boys in the OP had radioed in to say that they were in place.

Minutes later I heard footsteps coming towards me from the rear and turned round just as John tapped on the window. I opened the door and he sat down in the passenger seat, asking me if I was cold. Then he told me that he had just caught Rod with a blanket wrapped around him and had fined him £10. To me it seemed a small price to pay for some warmth. John checked that

I had my pistol with me, and the SMG, and that the maps were hidden from view. Then he told me to have a nice day, got out and walked off down the street.

A light came on in a house across the street and a woman's face appeared at the window. I called up on my radio to tell the others that someone was taking an interest in me and that I was preparing to move. I got out of the car to clear the ice from the windscreen and the woman in the house moved away from the window and turned off the light. It was so cold that I had to blow on my hands to keep them warm. At last the screen was clear and I turned the engine on, put the heater to maximum and pulled away.

I turned out into a main road, determined to drive for long enough to warm up the car and my frozen feet. As the ice on the rear screen cleared I could see that I was being followed and that it was a police car, complete with flashing blue lights. I had just enough time to radio in that I was being pulled over by the police before stopping and winding down the window.

The policeman got out of his car and came over to me, shining his torch through the open window. 'Is this your car?' he asked. There was no point in lying to him. If he checked the registration he would find that it was a blocked number and so I simply replied, 'No, it isn't.' He asked me to get out and I did so, trying to explain to him that it was a military vehicle. My explanation fell on deaf ears and he announced his intention of searching the car. I knew that this was a bad idea; I had a sub-machine gun on the back seat! I gave him a code word which, I told him, would explain my identity. He looked at me as if I were stupid and told me that I was being obstructive. His partner had, by now, got out of the car and come across. Thank God, I had managed to radio in the situation. At that moment John and Alistair arrived to rescue me. The policemen were obviously not happy to have three scruffy-looking individuals insisting that they were HM Forces and that they should check the code with the comms room. Eventually they did as we requested and we spent a tense five minutes waiting for an answer. Finally their radio came to life and I heard a voice telling them to back off immediately. I smiled weakly at them as they stomped back to their car and drove off, glaring at me as they passed.

After five long days the exercise came to an end and I was glad to get back to camp for a long soak in the bath. Christmas was nearly upon us and it was a pleasant surprise to be told that we were to be given a ten-day break for the festivities.

It was so good to go home again, but the time passed really quickly. I had a few awkward moments when asked what I had been doing and why I had grown my hair so long, but I managed to side-step the questions and had an enjoyable holiday.

Leanne picked me up from the railway station on the way back to camp. When we arrived we went into the bar, where Greg was holding court. It was obvious to us all that he was an officer. His cultured accent alone gave him away, and he had a habit of wearing a cravat solely to wind up the DS. This particular evening he had bought bottles of champagne to help us celebrate the fact that the course was almost over.

The following day we went straight back to surveillance in the city. Naturally the target was as slippery as an eel and we lost sight of him before very long. At the debriefing, Harry and Alistair poured scorn on our efforts. They told us that we would have to work a lot harder the following day as we would be helping another agency and they did not want us to show them up. They told us only that it was a government agency and that they would be testing their skills against those of the DS and of us. For this exercise we would be paired up with the DS, as they obviously had no faith in our ability to work alone.

I went off with Mike and Nick. The DS were tense. It was obvious that a lot of pride was at stake. The only clue we had been given was the registration number of a Toyota and we were told that our target was a man.

We spotted the car and began to follow it. Moving close behind, I could see that it contained two people with fluffy hair who were sitting quite low in their seats. They were obviously women. We tailed them into the city where we thought they would be meeting Bulls Eye One, the male target. They drove into a multi-storey car park and stopped. Then both women got out and were lost in the crowd before we had the chance to follow them. A short time later one of them returned to the car and drove off. We followed her this time and after a few minutes she stopped to pick up the other woman, before driving off again at speed. We lost the car once more, but Harry and Leanne found it after a frantic search. It was parked at the roadside and, since it appeared to be empty, Harry decided to see if he could break in. There was a blanket loosely thrown across the back seat, but Harry ignored it as he used a strip of flexible packaging to try to unlock the door. Suddenly the blanket on the back seat rose into the air and from beneath it appeared one of the women. She had removed her wig and her makeup was smeared, and, all at once, it was obvious that 'she' was a 'he'. Harry backed away, mumbling a garbled message which no one understood. As he looked on in disbelief, the cross-dresser started the car and drove off. It was the last we would see of him until the debriefing.

Back at base the government agency gleefully told us how easily we had been deceived. The target that we had been after had been the passenger in the car all the time. It had not occurred to any of us that the man might be dressed as a woman and none of us had got close enough to spot the deception. The man who had been dressed as a woman was fairly petite and told us that this disguise was one they often used. He advised us to adopt the same technique. We turned to look at the DS who were sitting rigidly at the back of the hall. The thought of Ted in a dress was a sight I did not want to contemplate!

The week of the last exercise finally dawned and we moved back to the city once more. That night an observation post was inserted and the long hours of surveillance and cover began. We worked for up to twenty hours a day and sleep became a luxury. I found it really hard to concentrate; my head was spinning with fatigue. The DS pulled back and left us to work as a team with the minimum of assistance. Our tailing had become quite slick. Without warning, while following the target through the city one day, the word 'Endex' came over the radio. That was it, the end of the exercise and the end of our training.

Packing up in silence, we made our way back to camp, each wondering what would happen next. The DS told us all to get a good night's sleep and to parade at eight am the following day.

The next morning we assembled to await our fate. The training major and Norman, clipboard in hand, appeared and told us to pay attention. Norman looked at the clipboard and called out some names, telling them to go to classroom two. The rest were told to follow him. Mark, Rob, Nick, Liam, Julia, Jamie, Greg, Leanne, Kate, Ben and I all marched off to classroom two.

We sat in silence in the classroom, hardly daring to breathe. At last Norman came into the room, his face impassive as ever, and made his announcement, 'You lot have been successful. Tomorrow morning you move out of here to your new postings.' With those few words he marched out and left us alone. The relief was enormous and there was a lot of back-slapping and hugging. Suddenly it all stopped as those who had not passed were made to march past our window. It was the final humiliation for Julian, Vince and the others. As he walked by Vince looked in and stuck his thumb up; the others looked straight ahead.

Julia, Leanne, Kate and I were elated. This was a first; four women had made it through the course on their own merits. It was certainly not the case that they were desperate for women, as we were soon to find out. We were each given new identity cards, fake Northern Ireland driving licences and car insurance documents. When I looked at mine I found that my name had been changed to Jackie Banks. Then Nina and Ted walked in and told us it was time for our briefing.

For the first time we were told we would be working for the 14 Intelligence Security Group (Northern Ireland) or 14 INTSYGP NI for short. We came to know it as the Det. It had been set up in the early 1970s as a security agency to monitor terrorist groups and was originally known as the Military Reaction Force or MRF. Initially it was composed of volunteers from various regiments, but was not a great success due to the lack of training. One of the worst failures came to be known as the 'laundry job'. A laundry had been set up in the Divis flats in Belfast as a cover to watch terrorist groups. The first woman ever to be used covertly in Northern Ireland was part of this operation, which ended with a fierce gun battle.

In the late 1970s the name of the unit was changed to 14 Intelligence Security Group. Officially the unit did not exist at all and the only place where the name could be found was on the door of a portakabin at headquarters in Northern Ireland. The unit itself was divided into three detachments, North, South and East, based in three locations. North detachment covered Londonderry, which was where Leanne, Ben and Greg were sent. Mark and Jamie went to the East detachment, which covered Belfast. The largest of the three detachments was the South, covering Armagh, Fermanagh, Co. Tyrone, Omagh and Co. Down. This was my destination, along with Kate, Julia, Liam and Rob.

We were told that, as part of 14 INTSYGP (NI), we would come under the control of the Royal Ulster Constabulary and that all our operations would be directed by the Head of Special Branch. Without his co-operation we would not be able to function. It was made clear to us that our training would continue 'over the water' and that there was still the possibility that one or more of us would be found wanting and would be sent home.

With this warning ringing in our ears we left the classroom and spent the remainder of the day packing our belongings. That night we went to the bar and got totally blasted!

CHAPTER TWELVE

The next day, our final day in England for some time, we drove to RAF Brize Norton, in Oxfordshire, to await darkness.

As the sun faded we were driven onto the airfield. There, at the end of the runway, a Hercules transport plane was waiting. It was a good old workhorse but not the most comfortable of aircraft. We sat on benches, clinging to cargo netting as the aeroplane lumbered down the runway and took off into the night air.

We were all still suffering from hangovers after the previous night and the only luxury we were allowed was a bucket. By the end of the flight it was full. We landed at Aldergrove airport and the Hercules taxied to a remote part of the airfield. The doors opened and we staggered unsteadily down the ramp at the back and climbed into the waiting vans. Then the van doors slid shut and we found ourselves in total darkness. We drove for an hour, squashed together with no fresh air. As usual the men thought they were being clever and amusing by farting every few minutes and soon the atmosphere was awful and tempers began to fray.

Eventually we stopped and the van doors were pulled open again. I was amazed to see that we were parked in a huge warehouse. Around the sides were a variety of cars and to my right were two portakabins, one on top of the other. I later discovered that this was the operations block. Straight ahead were more portakabins, built on raised blocks and stretched out in three rows.

I climbed down from the van and was immediately met by a well-built, dark-haired man with a daft grin on his face. 'Hello,' he said, 'you must be Jackie. I'm Rick, your new partner.' We were welcomed by the Commanding Officer who told us to get down to the bar and meet the rest of the Det.

Rick showed me the way to the bar, a large brick-built room which had been painted entirely black. It was packed with long-haired operators, or ops, all drinking beer from cans. Before we had the chance to settle down with a drink we were dragged off to join our respective Det groups. I managed a quick wave to Leanne before she disappeared with some others to North Det. Then a girl with blonde, wavy hair and clutching a gin and tonic came up to me and introduced herself as Becky. I recognized her; she was the horrible sergeant from Camp Alpha! She pulled me over to one side and began to give me the low-down on all the men. While she and I were talking, Julia came up to us and announced that it was nearly eleven o'clock and that we ought to be going. As soon as the words left her mouth I knew she was in trouble.

Becky looked her up and down and said, 'I hope you're not talking to me, darlin'. I'm not one of your girls.'

Julia turned crimson as she realized that pulling rank was not acceptable here. We stayed on in the bar until, eventually, Becky said she would drive us to our house.

Whilst the men were given accommodation in the warehouse, it had been decided that the women should be housed in Army quarters about a mile away. Becky had obviously lived in the house for some time and had it arranged to her taste. I am sure that she was not too happy about the arrival of three other women laden with boxes of belongings, but she said nothing. We soon found out that, although we had the house, we spent so much time at the Det that it was much more practical to sleep in a basha at the warehouse.

During our first few days in Northern Ireland we were kept busy making maps. Our area was so large that we had to have cut-outs, or small sections of maps, that could easily be handled in the confines of a car. When that task was complete we went on to choose our weapons. We had each been given two Browning pistols and a MP5K, but we also had the choice of an HK53 rifle with a folding stock or the more powerful G3 rifle. We kept the weapons in what was called the 'romper room', a locker room where we stowed all our kit. I found it rather unnerving to discover a bullet hole where a chap called Ross had had a 'negligent discharge', or ND, some weeks earlier.

We were allocated our cars. Mine was a Fiat Strada with three sets of false number plates, each relating to the counties in which we would be working. Each car had to be 'bleeped up', which meant being fitted with a covert radio and camera. The signals staff had to work around the clock to get everything sorted out for the new ops and the cars were virtually stripped out to install the wiring.

When it was all in place we had to do our road tests. The microphone for the radio was usually hidden in the air vents and the camera could be in a variety of places depending on the vehicle type and make. The test highlighted problems such as road noise on the radio and the correct angles for obtaining pictures with the hidden cameras.

In addition to the car radios we were also issued with personal radio sets. I spent two days adapting a shoulder bag to contain my radio, placing the inductor in the strap to boost the signal to my earpiece. The final piece of equipment to be issued was the medical kit, complete with the phial of morphine. That done, we were ready to get out on the road and familiarize ourselves with the area.

Rick took me out in his Escort. He had a terrific memory for car numbers, faces and locations, and as we drove along the country roads he pointed out houses belonging to suspected terrorists. I was nervous as we approached a small town. Groups of people stared at us as we passed and I knew that this was the town where, in 1968, the Catholic population had demonstrated for equal rights. Rick raised one finger to the onlookers and they nodded back to him. 'Don't forget to acknowledge them this way in Catholic areas,' he said, 'and remember to cross yourself when you pass a Catholic church.' I learned that a full hand signal was used in Protestant areas. It was small details such as these that could fool the locals into thinking you were one of them.

We drove on into Dungannon and Rick showed me the

Lisnahull estate, where some of our targets lived. For the first time I saw how the communities were divided, one street displaying the red, white and blue of the United Kingdom, the next the Irish tricolour. We had a huge area to cover and the orientation was difficult.

We went out every day and Rick would test me on the colours. Just when I was beginning to be comfortable with an area, we would move on to another. We went to Enniskillen, which took an hour and a half to reach, and then back through Omagh, Portadown or Craigavon. On our return we attended lectures given by the Sergeant in charge of the Intelligence Corps support team. We knew him as the 'Chief Spook' and he told us about previous operations and which terrorists were still active.

The day finally arrived when all the new ops had to prove themselves capable of surveillance. One of the old hands had to go out into the field and pose as a target for us to follow – a 'hare and hounds' exercise. We knew that however well we performed there would be criticism, especially of the women. From the start some of the men had made it clear that they hated women. One of them, Eddie, thought that all women were slags and should be kept in their places, tied to the kitchen sink. Lee, Ryan and Stan had all been in the previous intake of ops and thought it showed weakness to have a woman as a partner. Thankfully there were some men with a mature outlook who recognized the value of having women in undercover roles. Without them our lives would have been unbearable.

For the final test Rob, a chain-smoker who was never seen without a cigarette dangling from his mouth, was my partner. The target moved off and we followed with Rob at the wheel of the car. We soon found ourselves in Dungannon and noted that the target had stopped in a busy marketplace.

We were blocked in behind a bus until the driver indicated through the open cab window that we were clear to overtake. Rob turned the wheel and pulled out alongside the bus. As we drew level with the front, a small child ran out into the road and collided with the side of our car. I watched in horror as she bounced back into the road and landed on her bottom. We were on the outskirts of a hard Republican area called the Ponderosa and all around us were angry mothers fetching their children from school. It looked as if we were about to find ourselves in the middle of a very nasty situation.

The child did not appear to be badly hurt and we decided not to wait around any longer. I called in on the radio to report what had happened and Rob put his foot down hard on the accelerator and we took off. We went directly to the nearest police station where we spent a tense few moments at the security barrier. The police were obviously reluctant to let us in, as we looked so scruffy. Then Special Branch arrived and told us that the word on the street was that two British spies had deliberately knocked down a child. We went back to the Det. The car had been compromised and we had to change our appearances, but we had passed the test. Although we were no longer trainees, we continued to be known as the new ops until the next bunch arrived.

As the weeks passed we became very busy and were asked to conduct an operation in Location A. We were to set up an OP in the middle of the town in an old church which afforded excellent views of the targets as they moved around during the day. The order to move came unexpectedly one evening when we were all in the bar. We had been there for some time and had all had plenty to drink. Danny, the liaison officer, burst in and we could tell from the expression on his face that something was about to happen. The telephone rang and we were ordered upstairs for a briefing. We sat around in easy chairs as Danny looked at us all, trying to spot the most sober among the group. He selected Ryan and Nick to man the OP, with Rick and me making the drop-off.

We set off in a transit van with Rick driving. As he flung the van around corners I could hear the muffled grunts of the other two as they were thrown about in the back. It was the worst drop I ever experienced. We shot up the pavement and crashed into the fence. Rick and I were giggling uncontrollably as Ryan and Nick leapt out of the van and raced for cover. We drove off and waited for the message that they were in the OP and were up and running. It came after about two hours, by which time we were beginning to suffer from hangovers. At five am we drove back to the warehouse in a more sombre mood than when we had left.

Within a week the OP had been compromised when children began playing in the church. Ryan and Nick had to be extracted with the help of the police and the Quick Reaction Force, a regular army unit placed on standby for the operation. *An Phoblacht*, a Republican newspaper, reported the incident and took great delight in what they referred to as another victory for the IRA.

Despite this setback, the work continued. We went off to Enniskillen to allow things to settle in Location A. It was now June and the weather was hot. Every day Rick and I drove out to watch our targets, but they rarely moved. They were so lazy that we spent most of our time sitting beside a river or lake eating ice cream and sun-bathing. It was frustrating not having anything constructive to do and we were all anxious to get on with some real work.

Eddie, the op who thought that all women were slags, had been instructed to enter a target building in the town centre. Rick and I were to act as his cover and the operation was set for the early hours of one morning. Eddie, as team leader, decided that I should wear a skirt. I disagreed, as I was concerned that a skirt would hamper my chances of escaping should something go wrong. Eddie showed his true colours again, ranting and raving about women only being good for one thing, but I got my own way. Rick and I walked arm in arm down the road and stopped in a doorway for a cuddle. From this vantage point we could scan the entire street and shortly after our arrival we spotted Eddie and his companion Lee entering the target premises. The job went without a hitch and we were soon back in our warehouse. From that moment Eddie refused to speak another word to me and shortly afterwards he left the Det. We heard that his departure had something to do with his attitude!

The summer dragged on with nothing of any consequence happening. Then, as the days became shorter and the weather colder, we were suddenly pulled out of Enniskillen and sent back to Location A where there was an IRA active service unit. The information that had been received about this unit was that they intended to shoot a police officer.

Day after day we picked up the ASU members and followed them. I was surprised that they never seemed to notice that they were being followed. Sometimes Rick would drop me off in the town centre so that I could follow the targets on foot. They often congregated on a street corner next to a butcher's shop. I would stand in front of the butcher's window, shopping bag in hand and duffle coat clutched tightly around me while I listened to their conversation. It was in this sort of role that women were very effective. We just blended into the background. Between us, Becky, Kate, Julia and I spent many hours on the ground during the day. Our nights were spent on CTRs.

Around this time Rick left. I had known that his time in Northern Ireland was coming to an end and that he was due to return to his regiment. I dreaded him leaving as I would be left without a partner and, if no one volunteered to work with me, I would be out on a limb. The Army had decided that, although men could work alone, women had to have a partner. There was no logical explanation for this ruling. Since we had all undergone the same training it was not because women were less well equipped to cope with dangerous situations. It was simply another example of the inequality of treatment that the women had to suffer. It seemed that however well we performed we would always be regarded as inferior beings by the Army, and by many of the male soldiers too.

A number of new ops arrived at the Det. There was Derek, who had been in the Falklands, and Hugh, a small Cornishman who liked the ladies. He came from one of the tank regiments. We had a new man in charge, a soft-spoken Londoner called Steve, who was full of enthusiasm and wanted us to get out and do more jobs on our own. Unfortunately this attitude led to clashes with the Head of Special Branch and his cronies in Armagh. Joe became our Liaison Officer. His two passions were scuba diving and rugby. A lot of the old operators, including those who despised women, had left and some others had returned. One of the ops, who was back for a second time, was a woman called Kitty. She was a great character and was very experienced. She had been decorated for the work she had done before coming to Northern Ireland.

One afternoon Ray came over to speak to me. Everyone was slightly in awe of Ray. He was a Marine and had a distinguished career behind him. He had been with the Det since the MRF had been set up in the early 1970s and was one of the most experienced and respected operators. I wondered what he could possibly want to discuss with me, but I was also in awe of him and waited while he sat down at the bar, a gin and tonic in his hand. I was amazed when he said, 'I like you, woman. You and I would make a good team. Now, mine's a gin!' I had got myself a new partner.

Ray looked much older than I did and so we became the father and daughter team. He drove an old red Cavalier and smoked like a chimney. I had managed to get Rick to stop smoking in the car, although he still belched and farted. I knew that I had no chance of even suggesting to Ray that he stop smoking. His hard stare was just too much to endure.

The operation in Location A continued with us working long hours. Ray and I had only been together for a few weeks when we were sent out to cover a team on the ground. Other members of the Det were accompanied by a team from the SAS who were being shown how we worked.

Ray and I had stopped and were sitting listening to our radio when we heard Nick's voice shouting that he could see armed men walking across the moor less than a mile from where we were parked. We looked over and could see a car moving slowly along the road. I called up to find out where the other ops were. All the while the car was moving slowly towards us. It stopped about two hundred yards away and, in the moonlight, we could see the silhouettes of men carrying rifles get out and look around them. Satisfied that they were not being followed, they returned to the car which began its slow procession towards us once more.

This was really serious and I again shouted into the radio for everyone to stand by. Ray was holding his HK53; I had an MP5K in my hands and we had opened the car doors slightly. As the car came down the road its headlights caught the side of our car and Ray and I put our heads together in the classic courting couple pose. It turned into where we were parked and came to a stop. On Ray's shout of 'GO!' we leapt out of the car and aimed our weapons at the other vehicle. I had already released the safety catch when I heard a cry of, 'Jesus! Don't shoot!' It was Ross. Ray, his rifle still levelled at the car, yelled, 'Out,' and Ross, his face white as a sheet, tumbled out.

I could hardly believe how close we had come to opening fire. As Ross stood trembling, Ray gave him the biggest bollocking of his life. When he had finished he turned his attention to the SAS boys in the back and gave them the same treatment. We got back into our car and Ray lit another cigarette. His only comment on the entire situation was, 'Woman, you're all right!'

The long hours that we had been working in Location A began to pay off and we had built up a lot of intelligence on the ASU. They were sloppy and had no idea that they were being monitored. We found them easy to follow. We knew that they were about to move their weapons when, one night, Ray and I were parked on a country track. It was eerie sitting there in the dark, shrouded by the mist that rolled off the lough. Suddenly the target car pulled on to the track, headlights blazing. Ray and I were clutching our weapons, but we had nowhere to go. We again used the courting couple pose and the car pulled alongside ours and stopped. I lifted my head slightly and looked at our target. The driver had the car window open and was leaning out, leering at us and making crude gestures. I turned my head into Ray's neck and whispered, 'He's getting a cheap thrill.' Ray looked up and, in his best Irish accent shouted, 'Fuck off!'

Everyone in the target car laughed and the driver reversed back up the track. Had they challenged us with weapons I doubt that they would have known what had hit them. As it was they lived to fight another day, and so did we.

My partner, Ray, was coming to the end of his army career, but, before he left, was due for some well-deserved leave. He went off and, once more, I was left without a partner. Until Ray's return, Steve the boss decided that I should work with Kitty's partner, Kevin, as Kitty was also on leave. We had been doing such a lot of surveillance work in Location A that there was a very real danger of us being compromised. We constantly changed both our cars and our hairstyles, but it was still very risky and so it was decided that we should work mainly at night to minimize the chance of discovery and exposure.

Towards the end of September it was planned to set up another observation post to keep an eye on the ASU. We planned to insert it in a hedge close to where we had identified the unit's weapons hide. One evening we conducted a successful close-target recce and decided to insert the team the following night. I slept until the afternoon, having been up for most of the previous night, and spent the rest of the day getting ready for the job that night. There was nothing unusual, just kit to prepare, weapons to clean and magazines to re-load. Orders were scheduled for 22:30 hours.

Just before ten-thirty I walked into the briefing room and saw Kevin for the first time that day. He had been out during the afternoon and one look at him told me exactly where he had been. Kevin had not been blessed with very much hair and the little he did have was straight and usually flopped limply around his head. Tonight, however, it stood up on end like hundreds of tightly coiled springs.

I was silent for a moment and then, without thinking, exclaimed, 'What on earth have you done?' Kevin looked upset. 'It's a perm,' he said defensively, 'It's fashionable.' Ross walked in and began to laugh. 'Who's the poodle in the corner?' he wanted to know.

By now Kevin was really offended and told Ross that style was obviously something about which he was totally ignorant. Lee came into the room, his face streaked with green and black camouflage paint. He looked around and as he spotted Kevin and me he muttered sarcastically, 'You look like Bodie and fucking Doyle!'

The briefing began and by the time it had finished even the

police were making fun of Kevin and his hairdo. As soon as it was possible to leave the room, Kevin shot out of the door yelling to me over his shoulder, 'Let's go! We'll take the scenic route.'

We headed towards his car, a bright red Ford Capri. Lee was right. With his ridiculous perm and flashy car Kevin really did look like the television character and neither his hair nor his vehicle was a particularly good choice for a covert operation. We left the Det to shouts of 'Go get 'em, Doyle.'

We began our journey. Over the radio I could hear the call signs of the other vehicles as they moved off. We had left so quickly that they were at least ten minutes behind us as we sped along the country lanes that skirted the lough. This area was unfamiliar to me. Usually we kept to the 'A' roads before heading towards the motorway. I had to concentrate hard on my map, balancing it on my knee and using a pencil torch to follow the route we were taking. When I found our exact position I called over the radio that we were at Green Three Zero, towards Yellow Two Nine.

'What the . . . ,' Kevin began to speak and the tone of his voice made me look up. By the light of our headlamps I could see dark figures scuttling into the hedgerow. Ahead loomed a large dark shape. Kevin hit the brakes and my HK53 fell down and banged against my leg as he fought to control the nose-heavy car. I grabbed the stock as we skidded sideways and came to a stop, half on the grass verge. My pistol and the spare magazines dug into my back as I was hurled back into my seat. Then, because I was not wearing a seatbelt, I bounced forward again banging my head on the dashboard. Suddenly the car doors were opened and arms reached in, pulling me out of my seat and into the darkness. My head was spinning and I was losing my grip on the HK53. I could hear voices and one, with a strong Irish accent, shouted, 'She's got a gun.'

Someone pushed me to the ground and forced my face into the wet grass of the verge. I could smell the damp earth but was being held so tightly that I was unable to move. I was searched and my pistol was found. I tried to get up but only succeeded in raising my head, and was kicked in the face by a man wearing heavy black boots. Once more I heard the Irish voice, this time shouting, 'Get down, bitch!'

I had never been so frightened in my life as I was at that moment. My heart was pounding and my breathing uneven. I was sure that Kevin and I were going to die and no one even knew that we were in trouble. The whole situation had developed so quickly that there had been no chance to call on the radio and, because we had left in such a hurry and were so far ahead of the others, we might be dead before anyone reached us. I could hear the car being ransacked and then there were delighted shouts as they discovered Kevin's G3 rifle on the back seat. This was followed by the sound of Kevin's groans as they began kicking him.

I started to struggle and managed to free one arm. As I raised myself to my knees a bright light was shone into my face and I was instructed to stay still. I could see dark figures coming towards me and with my last ounce of strength I shouted at them, 'Security forces, you bastards.' It was a stupid thing to say but somehow it made me feel better.

I was kicked once more, this time in my back, and I fell forward into the grass. Hands grabbed my arms and held them in a vice-like grip. Then I was dragged into the road, my legs and feet following uselessly behind. My assailants pulled me upright and I saw them properly for the first time. Dressed all in black, they held carbines across their chests. One walked towards me, holding my false driving licence and army ID card and spoke to his companions. 'It's all right lads,' he said, 'they're on our side.' I could see that he was a sergeant from the Royal Ulster Constabulary.

I was released and the Sergeant placed a comforting arm around my shoulder. I turned to see Kevin being lifted to his feet, his face a mass of blood and dirt. We had just sat down on the bonnet of his Capri when the HMSU arrived. They had heard of the interception over the police radio and I thanked God that they had been made aware of our predicament. As they sped towards us they had confirmed over the radio that we were security forces and not IRA terrorists. The Sergeant told us that there had been a breakout that day from the Maze prison and that twenty IRA prisoners were on the run. There were police and army roadblocks everywhere but no one had thought to tell us about them. By driving on the country lanes instead of the A roads, we had accidentally come across a roadblock and when the police discovered our weapons they were sure that they had found two terrorists. When they saw Kevin's curly hair they were certain. His perm made him look exactly like one of the escaped prisoners.

We sat for a few moments collecting our thoughts and allowing our pounding hearts to resume their normal beats. Then we got back into Kevin's Capri and were slowly waved off by the police. I called over the radio to let the base know what had happened, but the boss had already been told and had decided to abandon the operation.

Some weeks later Special Branch identified an IRA unit in Location B. They wanted us to split our resources so that we could cover the surveillance of the unit in Location B while maintaining a watch on the ASU in Location A. It proved impossible, as we had insufficient manpower to cover both areas. Reluctantly, we were told to pull out of Location A and concentrate our efforts in Location B. After recent events I was delighted to be leaving Location A for Location B, a lively market town marred only by the dividing lines between Catholic and Protestant areas.

Our target in Location B was an IRA man named O'Donnelly who lived with his family in a cottage on a small estate. We quickly identified him. He was easy to follow, as he obviously had no idea he was being watched and he led us to many of his associates, some of whom had not been identified before. It was decided to break into his shed because it was thought it contained information of interest.

O'Donnelly's shed was to the side of his cottage and the only time that we had any chance of breaking in with the minimum risk of discovery was in the middle of the night. My partner Ray and I were picked for this unenviable task. We were dropped at the edge of the estate by a new op who we called Freddie. He had gained this nickname after someone remarked upon his likeness to Freddie Starr. He was from one of the tank regiments and was great fun. Later on he and I became good friends.

After Freddie dropped us off, Ray and I linked arms and walked into the estate. It was deadly quiet as we strolled towards O'Donnelly's house. From the moment we spotted the shed, I could tell that things would not go smoothly as there was a bright street lamp outside the cottage. We stopped for a moment and hugged each other, looking over each other's shoulders to check whether there was anyone about. It seemed unlikely at two am, but we had to make sure that the coast was clear. Ray moved quickly to the back of the shed. This was the worst time for me, standing alone in hostile territory in the middle of the night, gripping the butt of my pistol, which was in my duffle coat pocket. There was a dull clunk as he broke in then I heard Ray's muffled voice telling me that he was stuck. Peering around the corner I could see that his jacket was caught and, although he was frantically wriggling and trying to free himself, he was stuck fast. As if this were not bad enough, at that moment the lights came on in one of the rooms in O'Donnelly's house. I crouched by the side of the shed and told Ray to keep still. Then I heard raised voices coming from the cottage, only a matter of a few yards away from where we were trapped. Another light came on at the side of the cottage. The curtains were pulled back and there stood our target, shouting at a woman. Although we could not be seen from the cottage, I was worried that the shouting would attract the attention of the neighbours. If anyone from any of the houses around were to look out they would see us immediately. O'Donnelly moved towards the front door. I drew my pistol and crouched closer to Ray to tell him that the target was coming out. I passed the information over the radio and heard Freddie confirm that he was on his way to cover us. At that moment there was a loud ripping noise and Ray, his jacket badly torn, wriggled free. I grabbed his shoulder and helped him up. Then we linked arms once more and began walking away. At the end of the street we could see Freddie's Astra, the doors slightly ajar, ready for a quick get-away. We had only walked a few paces when the front door of the O'Donnelly residence flew open and the target headed towards his shed, shouting obscenities over his shoulder at the woman. He leapt into the car that was parked in front of it and drove off at speed.

By the end of October it was decided that the Army should apprehend the Active Service Unit members in Location A whose weapons hide we had been watching. So we left Location B and returned to Location A. During the early hours of the morning, Ray and I dropped off the Special team and raced back to the Det to get some sleep before we had to go out again to pick them up. At around three am two targets approached the weapons hide. Their driver remained in his car.

Our radio was quiet until, when Ray and I were about three-quarters of a mile away from the hide, we heard someone shout 'Contact, contact.' In the distance there was a burst of automatic fire. The two terrorists had aimed their weapons at the team who had told them to halt. When they ignored the warning the team opened fire, killing them both. Their driver sped off, but was injured and abandoned his car some distance away where he was rescued by IRA sympathizers who took him over the border to the south to have his wounds treated.

We cleared out of the area very quickly and returned to the Det in buoyant mood. The fact that three more terrorists were out of the way had to be very good news. They were always saying that they were in an armed struggle with the British and the way I looked at it was, if you live by the sword you die by it also. That night we had a party to celebrate. Looking back, it seems a strange thing to do when men had been killed. For us then it was simply a way of releasing the tension we had all felt that night. We knew that, had the result been different, they would not have shed a tear for any one of us.

CHAPTER THIRTEEN

Our work continued without a break. Sometimes we did two eight-hour shifts a day, seven days a week, and it would be between eight and ten weeks before we had a rest day.

We were still concentrating our efforts in hard Republican areas and the stress was beginning to get to us. At that time the army did not consider stress to be a problem that needed addressing, so we received no help at all. The only way to unwind was to drink. Our entire lives were centred around the warehouse; it was where we slept, ate and drank. We could go outside, but there was only one car we could use for socializing and so the opportunities were scarce. The male ops had their own portakabins or 'bashas' within the warehouse. We women had to share one and it had been decorated to Julia's taste; everything was in brown and orange. It was certainly not what I would have chosen, but no one really bothered about such unimportant things as interior design.

Just before Christmas, 1983, Headquarters decided to break into a premise belonging to an IRA suspect which they had somehow managed to obtain a key for. They gave us very little warning, but we went out and managed to locate the building. However, when we tried the locks we found they had been changed. We reported the situation back to Headquarters and were told not to make a fuss; a technician would be sent that evening for a recce. A small number of ops were trained in what was euphemistically known as 'methods of entry'. To an outsider it would have been called housebreaking and these ops were highly skilled in picking door locks.

That evening two men arrived. They were both sporting designer clothes and one stood out like a sore thumb. He was wearing white trousers, a red jumper and a cravat. He was immediately given the name Rupert! He and his companion attended the briefing. Liam, who was in charge of the operation and had been picked to break into the house, asked Rupert if he would like to change before we set off. A look of amazement crossed his face as Rupert replied that he was ready to go immediately. 'Not dressed like that, you're not!' said Liam.

Someone found a large pair of combats and Rupert was bundled into them. He insisted on wearing his cravat, which, unfortunately, did nothing to enhance his appearance. Liam continued with the briefing. When he reached the part about weapons he looked over at Rupert and asked him if he had passed the course for 9mm handguns. Rupert looked down his nose and said with a sneer, 'Of course I did'. Rupert was issued with a 9mm pistol at the end of the briefing and he, Alan and Liam piled into the back of the transit van. Ray and I had been chosen to drop them off at the house. As we pulled out of the compound we heard Alan bellowing at us to stop and we immediately pulled over. The side door slid open and out got Alan. He had Rupert by the scruff of the neck and he propelled him towards the Det. Rupert was clutching the pistol and it appeared that the safety was off. It amused me to hear Alan muttering, 'Typical officer, bloody useless,' as he frogmarched Rupert away. The pistol was taken away from Rupert and he and Alan returned to the van. I heard later that Rupert had been waving the pistol about in the back of the van with the slide pulled back and the safety off. He was heard to complain that it was not as good as a Lee Enfield.

Back on the road again, we sped off towards the house. The team had been keeping watch and we were happy when they reported that there was no one in. We made our drop directly in front of the building and I could see Alan and Liam dragging Rupert into the darkness. Ray and I went off and parked to wait for the call to pick up the intrepid team and take them back to our warehouse.

After about two hours we were relaxing with a cup of coffee.

Ray had just lit another cigarette when the message came over the radio that the team needed to be picked up immediately. Liam's voice sounded very tense and we raced off to fetch them. As we pulled up they emerged from the shadows. Rupert was in the middle. His face was bleeding and he was covered in dust. Alan bundled him into the transit and climbed in after him. Through the hatch I asked what had happened. Alan's reply made Ray roar with laughter and he had to stop the van in case he drove it off the road. Nick, at the other end of the radio, wanted to know what was happening and I had to tell him that Rupert had fallen down the stairs and broken a table and smashed a vase. For a moment there was nothing but silence as the information was digested; then the radio crackled to life again. This time it was Joe, our liaison officer, who told us, 'They want it to look like a burglary, so get back to the house and nick something!'

To make it look realistic Liam and Alan kicked down the door this time and returned to the van a few moments later with a television, some silverware and assorted electrical items. We drove back to the Det and everyone turned out to see Rupert emerge from the van still covered in dust. We took the stolen items into the bar and decided to put them up as prizes in our Christmas raffle. Then we sat down for the drink that Rupert bought for us. We were beginning to unwind when the door was suddenly pushed open and in walked LB, who was the right-hand man of our police boss at HQ. LB was our nickname for him; it stood for 'Lying Bastard'. The expression on his face told us that he was furious. He looked at our loot and muttered, 'Incompetent idiots. Don't think that you can keep this lot either.' With that he strode out again and everything that we had taken from the house was handed over to the police.

My partner Ray left and we heard later that he had been decorated. My new partner was a quiet man called Derek. Quiet that was unless he had a few Bushmills inside him, when he became a lunatic, stripping off his kit and dancing naked on tables.

After the success we had had in Location A, Steve was anxious to get back to work and to keep the initiative on our side. The

IRA was still smarting from the loss of volunteers and all our Dets were kept very busy.

Earlier in the year the North Det was operating in the hard Republican area of Location C. Two ops were in an OP close to a target house. At around eight pm one evening an IRA unit approached the rear of the OP and before the ops had the chance to do anything shot them both, killing Sergeant Baxter and severely injuring his partner. One of the ops had managed to shout 'Contact' into his radio before he had been shot and, within minutes, the ground team had arrived at the scene. They swarmed across a field towards the OP and, finding that the terrorists were still on the scene, began firing and managed to kill three IRA men. The observation post was quickly extracted and, despite massive injuries, the second op survived.

The death of Sergeant Baxter really shocked us, but the police hardly gave us time to even think about our loss, as they wanted us back in Location A to work against another terrorist unit. Within days of being back on the streets of Location A we had been compromised. These terrorists were not stupid and immediately spotted strangers in their midst. Although we changed the cars and our appearances it was felt that we should be pulled out for a while to let things settle.

The place chosen for our retreat surprised us all, as we were sent to Portadown, a mainly Protestant area. Special Branch believed that there were weapons buried somewhere on waste ground near the famous Gavaghy Road and they wanted us to find them.

The hunt began and night after night teams went out on to the streets looking for the weapons hide. It was like looking for a needle in a haystack. One night, quite by chance, one of our cars was passing a pub car park and saw a group of men acting suspiciously. They were loading the boot of a car with long, narrow objects that appeared to be wrapped in blankets. The ops decided that it was worth keeping an eye on the car as it left the car park. They followed it all the way to Armagh, where it stopped outside a large house in the Protestant area of the city. Joe, the liaison officer, was in Armagh himself at the time, with

Special Branch, and was keeping them informed of the situation.

Derek and I had been sent in to keep watch and we parked across the road, pretending to be a courting couple. There was no doubt in our minds that these people were Protestants and, judging by the area, were quite wealthy. We had been sitting there for a few minutes when the door to one of the houses opened and out came a number of men wearing smart suits. They opened the boot of the parked car and looked inside. They seemed delighted with what they saw.

At that moment the driver ran out of the house, jumped into the car and drove off at speed. Something was obviously not going according to plan. The men in suits rushed over to their own cars, climbed in and took off behind the first car. Before we had the chance to follow them an urgent voice came over the radio telling us to pull off immediately. Derek and I looked at each other, hardly able to believe what we had heard. The voice belonged to Joe and, since he was with Special Branch in Armagh, it appeared that the order to back off had come directly from them.

We drove back to base and found Steve in an absolute rage. Joe was already there, having been brought back from Armagh by helicopter. We sat down for a debriefing.

The scene that we had witnessed had been an exchange of weapons between Loyalist terrorists. When Joe had reported the events to Special Branch he had been completely unprepared for their furious reaction. He, like us, thought that we had all done a good job in locating these terrorists, regardless of their political persuasion. However, it seemed that the Royal Ulster Constabulary was only concerned with apprehending Republican terrorists. We were told in no uncertain terms that we were never to work that area again. They also made it clear that they expected us to treat the evening as if it had never happened and under no circumstances were any records to be kept. The driver of the car containing the weapons had driven off in a hurry at a point when it seemed as if a leisurely exchange was about to take place. Could it be possible that he had been tipped off about us? If that were true there can only have been one source of the information. It was a frightening thought.

I believed that I had been sent to Ireland to help bring terrorists to justice and to make it a safer place in which everyone, Protestant and Catholic alike, could live. Of course I knew that the RUC recruited almost entirely from among the Protestant population, but surely the police were meant to be impartial. How on earth would the situation ever change if a police force, entrusted to keep the peace between all sections of society, actively pursued Republican terrorists whilst turning a blind eye to the actions of the Protestants?

After the incident in Armagh we found ourselves with very little to do. We spent a lot of the time training and, in particular, improving our surveillance skills, but it was April before we had another job. Joe came back late one evening after a meeting with Special Branch and briefed us on what they wanted us to do.

Information had been received about a possible terrorist attack in Location D. We were given a couple of names and addresses and told to get on with it. Steve made it clear that he wanted a good result from this operation and that, to achieve this end, we would each be required to work two eight-hour shifts per day.

The area was, of course, Republican and was dotted with small villages and narrow lanes. It was the ideal places for IVCPs. The Green Army did not patrol regularly and the locals regarded strange cars with suspicion.

Our targets lived in a small village in the surrounding countryside, which made surveillance a nightmare, although it was a good area in which to insert OPs. We decided that it would be best to use a helicopter to follow the target cars during the day and only use cars ourselves after dark.

Each op was supposed to take a turn in the helicopter, but in practice that rarely happened. It was not a popular duty. Some ops made the excuse of feeling sick, whilst others just openly refused to fly in a helicopter. Invariably the women manned the helicopter. Being stuck for three and a half hours at a time in a freezing-cold Gazelle was not my idea of a good way to spend a weekend. The Army did not believe in luxuries such as heating and, in spite of thermal underwear, you became chilled to the bone in a very short time.

I seemed to spend a lot of time on helicopter duty, day after day, hour after hour, peering through the Perspex bubble, trying to follow what was happening on the ground. Although it was springtime, the weather was bad and often, before we landed, the fog would come down, making it impossible to see anything. The bad weather frightened me as it meant that we had to fly entirely on instruments. I hated not being able to see anything but cloud in front and would keep my eyes on the instruments to make sure that we were still flying straight and level. There was always the chance that we would crash into a pylon or a mountain and in my mind I would see these obstacles looming out of the mist and coming up to destroy us. It was always a great relief when we broke out of the cloud. Even when the weather was a little better it was boring. Sometimes the target cars did not move for hours on end and we would sit in the Gazelle, hovering around waiting for something to happen. When the weather was clear it could be quite exciting to skim along at treetop height, flying past the target and taking photos. The pilots loved hedge-hopping and their manoeuvring skills never failed to amaze me.

The actual duty of the op assigned to the helicopter was to watch the target, map-read and pass all relevant information to the team below. It was not easy to do.

The search for the IRA team continued through April and May, but by June we had identified them and had also located their weapons hide. Derek and Hugh spent many hours during the dead of night painstakingly removing the weapons and photographing every stage of the operation so that everything could be replaced in exactly the same way. Sometimes they would hand the guns to me and I would take them to the nearest secure base to be examined by a weapons expert.

Back at the hide Derek and Hugh would anxiously await my return so that they could replace everything. On many occasions I rushed back to them with the weapons just as dawn was breaking. It was a nerve-wracking time as they patiently put it all back together.

Whenever he had some significant information, the Head of

Special Branch, would come to the Det to brief us. He was a tall man who had worked his way up through the ranks. He had had his fair share of problems during the troubles and carried the scars of a couple of bomb blasts to which he had been too close. He was not a particularly likeable man but was more pleasant than his right-hand man, LB, who was disliked by us all.

The day of the attack arrived. The Head of Special Branch arrived for the briefing and puffed away on a cigarette while LB told us that the target was to be a house in the Location D. The terrorists planned to plant an explosive device in the house. LB then told us that we would no longer be required as another unit was going to finish the job. All the ops turned to look at the other unit boss who was sitting at the back of the briefing room. He shifted uncomfortably in his seat. Having completed his briefing LB followed the Head of Special Branch out of the room and straight to the bar where, to add insult to injury, they proceeded to drink our booze without paying for it. Steve was again furious and vowed that after all our hard work we would not be railroaded off the operation.

In the end it was decided that the Army Unit should go in on the ground with the Det in full support. A chap called Ferret would be leading the Army Unit team. We would provide a car team and the helicopter for which I was nominated, along with a pilot named Phil. We were to wait at the army base and would only become airborne if a firefight ensued. Should that happen the helicopter could illuminate the area with a powerful searchlight called a Nightsun, which was equivalent to one million candle power. We stripped the helicopter of everything that was not absolutely necessary. If the operation resulted in casualties we would need the space to transport the injured.

Late one evening a team from the Det dropped off the Army Unit lads close to the intended target. Phil and I sat waiting on the heli-pad in Dungannon. Both doors had been removed from the helicopter and the wind was blowing through the cabin. Just before midnight we received a radio message telling us that armed men had been seen crossing a field near to where the team had been dropped. I looked across at Phil and nodded to him. The rotors began to turn and we were lifting off as we heard the call 'Contact, contact,' over the radio.

The next message was from Ferret shouting for us to get there as quick as possible as one of the terrorists was trying to get away. Within minutes we could see the lights of Location D but had no idea of the team's exact position. To help us find them Ferret turned on a flashing beacon which guided us towards the field.

We banked steeply and Phil turned on the nightsun. The seat harness dug into my chest as we turned and I had the HK53 up to my shoulder as I scanned the fields below. Phil was worried that trees or pylons would damage the helicopter but Ferret was urging us to fly in lower towards the house. Below me I could see one of the Army Unit team standing over a body on the ground. As we turned once more the light swept over the road where a man stood, hands held high. He seemed to be rooted to the spot. Phil was by now very agitated as we were flying at rooftop height and were an easy target for the terrorists. It would be an enormous coup for them if they managed to shoot down a helicopter. He decided that we had been there long enough and turned off the light and pulled away, banking and weaving towards safety.

Once we were away from the scene, Phil and I sat in silence listening to the chatter on the radio. We heard that one IRA man, Patrick Neil, had been killed and two others had been arrested by the Army. In the search that followed, weapons and explosives had been found. Everyone went back to the Det in party mood.

After the Army unit had been debriefed they joined the rest of us in the bar. Only Phil was missing, as he had taken the helicopter to be serviced. He flew back in a replacement and came looking for me. 'They found a bullet strike on the tail,' he said. 'Some fucker had a go at us!'

He was obviously shaken and a mental picture of us plunging to the ground flashed before my eyes. We had been very lucky. Special Branch was pleased with the operation..

The next task dreamed up for us by Special Branch was probably the stupidest thing we had ever been asked to do. LB had been given some information that a man with strong IRA sympathies was having an affair with a woman he worked with at a factory in Omagh. The affair was carried on in a delivery van parked somewhere in a lay-by. When Joe came back from Special Branch to tell us what was planned we were stunned.

We were supposed to find the delivery van and then wait for the couple to get inside. Having allowed them a few moments to start doing whatever it was they had gone there to do, we were supposed to break in and take photos of them. Armed with these compromising pictures, the Police hoped they would be able to blackmail the man into giving them information. We could not believe they were serious. Joe shrugged his shoulders and said, 'Yes, I know. It's a crap job but it's all they will give us.'

We spent a week driving backwards and forwards along the main Omagh to Dungannon road but in all that time never managed to catch a glimpse of the delivery van. We gave up looking and Special Branch never mentioned it again. It was time for us to move on.

CHAPTER FOURTEEN

We went back to Location A after Special Branch received a tip off that a new ASU was being formed there. This time the players were all experienced IRA men; some had even served prison terms for murder. The police were worried, as these were ruthless men capable of all kinds of atrocities.

Our job was to get as close as possible to the unit and to gain as much information about them as we could. We were given information that they were plotting and scheming for what was known as a 'spectacular'. The plan was to hit an off-duty soldier from the Ulster Defence Regiment as he left his house. Because we knew their intentions we did not need to follow them at all and they remained convinced that they were not under suspicion.

Once we knew when the attack was planned we had to move fast. The operation promised to be a difficult one as UDR officers, like those of the RUC, lived and worked out in the community. Just days before it was due to take place we discovered the identity of the target. The soldier lived in an isolated house, quite close to Location A. Special Branch immediately appointed a team to watch him day and night.

We at the Det were tasked with setting up a number of OPs along the road. We knew the road on which the attack was planned but had not discovered at which point it was due to take place. By the date on which the attack was planned numerous OPs had been set up and manned and a large Army team had been deployed in vehicles on the ground. Gavin, who was one of our operators, and I had hired an HGV which we were to drive along the route normally taken by the UDR soldier.

Minutes before the soldier would normally have left home to travel along the road Gavin and I started out in the HGV. The height of the cab gave us a good view over the hedgerows and we drove slowly, trying to spot the signs of an IRA ambush. We saw nothing, so I radioed for the driver to move off. Another Army soldier, Buster, and his team of three followed him in a Fiat. Gavin parked the lorry and we sat listening to the radio as the two cars moved off down the road.

Almost at once things started to go wrong. A bread van pulled out of a garage forecourt in front of Buster's Fiat and then accelerated past the decoy driver's car. As it passed them they realized that it had nothing to do with delivering bread as the rear doors opened and two men clutching Armalite rifles began shooting at them. Immediately Buster and his team sped off after the van but bullets hit their car and the radio went down. The Army were using their own network and we could not access their radio channel. Our own network was alive with ops all wanting to know what was happening. The van, a Ford Escort, was hurtling along the road closely followed by the Army team, fierce gunfire coming from both vehicles. It was clear that the Army soldiers' MP5Ks were no match for the terrorist's Armalites.

By this time Gavin and I had decided that we should also be involved and so we trundled back along the main road as fast as we could go in a heavy lorry. Ahead of us the Escort skidded round a bend, closely followed by the Fiat. We had all passed a local garage when a civilian, appearing from nowhere, was caught in the crossfire and was hit. He died at the scene.

We saw the back end of the Escort turning left on to a minor road underneath the motorway but knew that we had no chance of catching it as it headed back towards Location A. The Army were also unable to follow as their car was badly damaged and skidded past the turning, coming to a stop. Gavin and I pulled alongside the car and I was horrified to see all the bullet holes around the engine. Amazingly, all four soldiers were unharmed but were badly shaken. We followed the Fiat back. It took a long time as smoke was pouring from the engine and we were not sure if it would make it back to camp. The duty regiment on the gates stood open-mouthed as they waved through the bullet-ridden car. Not a word was spoken. The recriminations started at the debriefing.

The IRA had got their spectacular and an innocent civilian had been killed. Special Branch was furious and wanted to know why Gavin and I had not spotted the terrorists' van when we drove along the road. Steve, our boss, jumped up and pointed out that, at the time we had driven past, the van was parked on the garage forecourt, out of sight. LB then turned his attack on the Army, criticizing them for not being able to shoot straight. Both he and the Head of Special Branch had to beat a hasty retreat as Buster let them have a mouthful of abuse.

The entire operation had been a fiasco. We had been using different radio channels, so that when the trouble started no one knew what was happening. The other soldiers were not familiar with the area and were too far behind during the chase. Perhaps the most frustrating thing of all was that our ops in the observation posts could see what was happening. They had had time to get down to the road to fire on the van from the front, but they were under the strictest of orders from Special Branch to stay where they were and could do nothing but watch helplessly.

There were bad feelings all round and Special Branch took particular delight in telling us that the IRA unit were already celebrating their success and were planning more jobs, now that they had witnessed the ineffective way we had opposed them. Steve and Joe argued with Special Branch that we should all be back in Location E working against them and eventually, after much discussion, we were given the go-ahead.

The Army licked their wounds and started to come out with us again to get to know the area. It was difficult for them as they only spent six months at a time in Ireland, so it was not possible for them to be as familiar with the countryside as we were. Some of their officers were not happy about them mixing with us anyway and tried to keep the joint excursions to a minimum. Thankfully, other officers realized the value of this mixed training and encouraged it. We worked long days and nights in Location

E, building up intelligence on the ASU and on others who were previously unknown to us.

I had recently been promoted to Lance Corporal and, in the autumn, was summoned to our headquarters in Lisburn. The boss at HQ, a full Colonel known to us as Wally, told me I had to think of my future. At some point I had to return to the Green Army. Becky had already left and had been sent to Hong Kong. I had had a couple of letters from her telling me how much she hated it there. I knew I would have to leave sometime. The Boss told me that there was a course coming up in Catterick on which there were vacancies and that, afterwards, I could have the pick of any posting. Without really thinking what I was saying, I replied, 'I quite fancy Hong Kong.' 'Leave it with me,' he said, and that was it; I had a few short weeks left in Northern Ireland and then I would be on my way to Hong Kong.

Suddenly a place was found for me on an educational course that all NCOs have to take. It lasted for four weeks and covered communication skills, maths, man management and the role of the Army in the contemporary world. I hated every one of those four weeks. It was strange to be back in a classroom, wearing jeans and a sweater while all the other participants sat there in their uniforms wondering who I was. Only the chief instructor knew my real identity and he was quite happy when, after a phone call, I would disappear for the rest of the day to do an eight-hour stint back with the Det. The WRAC officer who taught the course took an instant dislike to me and made many attempts to discover my identity. On the day of the exams she came up to me and said, 'I don't know why you bothered coming here.' I never saw her again but I know that she would have been furious when she found out that I passed the course with distinction.

During my time on the course the Det had started to get some good results. They had found some weapons hides and Special Branch was pleased. There had been a tip off that an IRA unit was going to try to set up the RUC and the Green Army. They planned a bomb hoax at Brennan's Barn, a hotel restaurant in Fermanagh near to the town of Enniskillen. This was not a new tactic. Many hotels at the time received hoax bomb warnings.

This time, however, the plan was slightly different. The hotel would be telephoned and told that there was a bomb. They of course would alert the security forces who would be caught in a bomb blast, which would be activated by the IRA unit as they raced to the hotel.

As with most information of this type, it was received at the last moment and was imprecise. Two teams were initially deployed in Fermanagh. We had not been told in which road the bomb would be planted and we had no idea what type of bomb would be used. A third team of ops and one from a Special Army team went to the police station at Portadown to wait. The Army team were briefed to stop the bombers and we were told to stay away until the bomb had been found. It was a bitterly cold day.

The informant was supposed to call Special Branch with more details but nothing had been heard from him and things were becoming fraught. Since we had not been able to pinpoint the exact area where the bomb had been planted, the teams went out in cars to begin the search. At the eleventh hour we were told by Special Branch to look out for a brown car. That was it; there would be no more information.

We had been on the ground for twelve hours and were cold and hungry. Derek and I drove slowly along the narrow lanes, our vision obscured by patches of thick fog. Then a voice over the radio shouted that a brown car had just passed his lie-up point. Next came a call from one of the Army team to say that the car had just passed them and that they were in pursuit. Joe informed us that the Brennan's Barn had received a telephone call warning them that a bomb had been planted. The caller had given a code word that had been recognized and the hotel was being evacuated. Everyone started to move in towards the hotel, each of us conscious that we could be blown up at any moment.

Derek suddenly braked hard and there, in front of us in the road, lay a black cable. I called in this information and Steve's voice came back over the air telling us to deal with it. We got slowly out of the car, both carrying our HK53 machine guns. Derek picked up the cable and we began to follow its course into a field. If this was the command wire, leading to a bomb, we were in a no-win situation. We could either be walking towards the bomb and a distinct possibility of being blown sky high, or we could be heading away from it, in which case we would be going directly towards the IRA bombers, who would be waiting to detonate the device.

All at once from across the field came the sound of gunfire and a flare shot high into the air, illuminating the area with an eerie blood-red glow. Then came the familiar call over the radio of 'Contact, contact' and Derek and I turned and ran back to our car.

Corporal Paul Worsley of the Special Army team and his companion had blocked in the brown car with their own vehicle, but by a tragic coincidence they had stopped the car directly in front of a hedge in which the IRA bombers were busily preparing their bomb. Hardly able to believe their luck, the terrorists had shot Paul in the back.

Derek and I were, at this point, hurtling towards the scene not knowing what had happened. The fog was beginning to clear and the sky was lit by many flares and the occasional bursts of tracer. We skidded to a halt and found ourselves behind Paul Worsley's car. In the confusion ahead, three IRA terrorists escaped, heading for the border with Eire a few miles away. When the firing stopped someone shouted, 'Man down, man down,' and familiar figures began running in our direction. In the shadow of the hedgerow we could just make out a shape which turned out to be Paul Worsley's body. An eerie silence descended on the area and Derek and I remained where we were, scanning the fields and hedgerows for any signs of movement.

We worked very hard to save Paul but he had been shot at very close range with a high-calibre weapon and there was nothing we could do for him. Eventually the Green Army and the police arrived, complete with helicopters clattering overhead. Several milk churns were found, packed tight with explosives, powerful enough to make a huge crater in the road and kill anyone who happened to be close at the time.

This was another night of despair for us and the drive back to camp seemed endless. Neither Derek nor I spoke, each of us lost in our own thoughts of another friend who had been lost.

Christmas came and, to cheer us all up, Kitty suggested that we have a theme party. It was decided that it would be a Western theme and would include a sheep roast and lots of beer. Obtaining the beer was not a problem; the sheep proved more difficult. Eventually we sent out a couple of the lads to rustle some lambs. Unfortunately it had not occurred to anyone that lambs are rather thin on the ground in December and the rustlers came back with an ancient ewe that they had shot. The sheep died in vain as the meat proved to be totally inedible. Undaunted by that small setback, we decorated the bar with bales of hay and a couple of picnic benches that one of the teams had 'liberated' from a local beauty spot.

The other Dets were all invited and North Det arrived in spectacular style with Mad Monty driving a Mini Metro into the bar. The bar doors were not as wide as the car but Monty had never been one to let a small detail like that deter him. Our other guests included the bosses from HQ. It appeared that they had not quite grasped the finer points of a theme party. They all arrived wearing smart suits and became the butt of endless practical jokes. Sometime during the evening they stood up next to the buffet table to thank us all for our efforts during the past year. While the speech was in progress one of the lads lit a flash bang and dumped it in a large bowl of curry. Within seconds there was an explosion which sent showers of curry raining down over the officers. They tried to maintain their dignity but it is not an easy task to look dignified with a dollop of vindaloo hanging off the end of your nose!

The evening progressed with Josh, the Sergeant in charge of the signals support team, setting fire to a bale of hay. He had been sitting on a bale in a drunken stupor when the idea came to him and he continued to sit there, engulfed in smoke and with a stupid grin on his face as the fire took hold. The fire had to be put out and we all grabbed fire extinguishers and hose pipes and enthusiastically tackled it. Once Josh was out of danger it seemed like a good idea to continue fire-fighting and our ops took on the boys from the Regiment. Soon the bar was awash.

The following morning we were given an early call by Ken, who was in charge of the day-to-day running of the Det. No one dared to disobey him. The bar had to be cleaned and, armed with mops and buckets, we set about the task, stopping only to remove a very wet but comatose Josh from the debris.

We had had a good time and the party had taken our minds off the terrible events of the previous few days. The married ops went off home for the Christmas break and, when they returned just before New Year, it was my time to leave. All my belongings were packed in boxes and I went round saying goodbye to everyone. I dissolved into tears more than once as I hugged them all. I had made many good friends and it was hard to leave them. But I was going back to the real world at last.

CHAPTER FIFTEEN

When my leave was over I went back to 8 Signals Regiment at Catterick Garrison. Packed in my suitcase was the green uniform I had not worn for two years. I was delighted to see that Des and Sarah, friends from my initial training, were also taking the course with me.

The first morning was awful. We gathered on the Parade Square and were inspected by an officer and a sergeant. I had not had to do this sort of thing for a very long time and it felt strange to stand to attention in my uniform.

Then it was back to the classroom with a vengeance. There was so much to take in as most of the procedures and equipment had changed since I had last worked with the Signals. I was so out of date that I just looked blankly at the textbooks in front of me. At the end of the first lesson the Sergeant, a gaunt Yorkshireman, took me to one side. 'Right lass,' he said. 'I know what you've been up to these past two years. Keep your head down and listen. You'll soon pick it up again.'

The course was difficult. There was so much to learn and I hated the old 'yes, Sir, no, Sir!' routine, so typical of the Army. The stress of the whole situation was really getting to me and I developed an eating disorder. I spent a fortune on chocolate, forgoing proper food. It was all I ate and very soon my weight started to creep upwards. Strangely, I found great comfort in eating like this. At least this was something over which I still had control.

One morning, when I was supposed to be at a parade I stayed in bed. It was too much trouble to get up. Des also stayed away and, of course, the duty Corporal caught us both. She made us parade before her that evening in our best tunics. As she came up to me she deliberately stood on my foot, making my best shoes dirty. Without thinking I grabbed her by the throat and pushed her up against the wall, knocking her forage cap to the floor. She looked terrified as I warned her never to mess me about again. Des was rooted to the spot. 'What on earth have they done to you?' she wanted to know. I released my grip on the Corporal and she rushed out of the room.

I was ashamed at the way I had behaved towards her, but I also knew that I was doing what I had been taught to do. Over the water I had had to react to each situation in a split second. Everything had to be second nature to me because terrorists rarely give you another chance. Having lived and worked that way for so long I found it very difficult to forget my training and behave like the person I had been before I went to Ireland. The Army had taken great care to ensure that all uncover ops knew how to behave in dangerous or provocative situations. However, once that function had been fulfilled they had no interest in any rehabilitation that might be necessary. We were left to cope as best we could and, to make matters worse, we were not permitted to tell anyone what we had been doing, so could offer no explanation for seemingly aggressive behaviour.

I managed to complete the course without any more nasty incidents. When it ended I had just one week left in this country before taking up my posting in Hong Kong. Freddie, my best friend from the South Det, came over and we spent the week touring around the Cotswolds. Then he took me to Gatwick airport to catch my flight. Suddenly the last place I wanted to go was Hong Kong. As I went through the departure gates I turned, waved to Freddie and promptly burst into tears. I wanted to be back at the Det with people who understood me and where, curiously enough, I felt safe in spite of the ever-present dangers. The flight passed by in an alcoholic blur as I downed gin and tonics one after the other.

Becky was waiting for me at Kai Tak airport. 'Welcome to Honkers, love,' she said as she guided me out of the building and into her car. 'You look like you need a drink!' She drove me to my new home, HMS *Tamar*, which was situated in a prime position on Hong Kong Island, overlooking the harbour. I was jet-lagged and had a raging hangover, but we dropped off my luggage and Becky whisked me away to the city and into the nearest decent bar.

Suddenly it was like coming home. Barry, one of the officers from North Det, was in the bar and the three of us sat drinking beer and talking over old times. I was pleased to learn that Captain T, who had encouraged me to volunteer for Project Alpha, had been promoted and was now the Major in overall charge of all the women in Hong Kong.

The Signal Squadron to which I had been posted was responsible for the biggest tape relay centre in the Far East. The centre was underground and for fourteen hours each day, four days a week, we worked like slaves, running round the machines which spewed out endless tapes. When each shift was finished we had to climb sixteen floors up to our accommodation.

The block in which we lived was air-conditioned but most of the time it was very humid and quite uncomfortable. There were also other problems in the building. One morning I was horrified to find a Chinese worker, wearing a gasmask, prowling around my room. He had what appeared to be a flame-thrower on his back. I sat bolt upright in bed and the sudden movement startled him. 'Missy, cockies, cockies,' he said by way of an explanation. 'Oh, God,' I thought, 'a pervert,' and told him in no uncertain terms what to do with himself. He backed out of the room, bowing and still muttering, 'Cockies, cockies.' At that moment my roommate, Linda, came in and I told her what had happened. She fell about laughing. My 'pervert' was only fumigating the building, which was infested with cockroaches. As if to prove the point, a huge cockroach dropped out of the air-conditioning duct and landed on the floor at my feet. It was enormous. I did not know whether to stamp on it or use it as a skateboard. Linda made the decision for me by whacking it with one of her boots. It died with a sickening crunch.

Like many of the girls, I was homesick at first, but, since I was in Hong Kong, I was determined to make the most of it. Between each four-day shift we had four rest days and I used this time to explore as much of the country as I could.

Hong Kong was wonderful – an unusual mixture of towering modern skyscrapers and old Colonial houses. I had never seen so many people before. The streets were teeming with life and never seemed to sleep. Sometimes a group of us would go out at night to visit the markets. They sold everything: cameras, electrical goods, fake 'designer' clothes, all at ridiculously cheap prices.

We often finished our shopping trips with a meal in the market. There you could select your fish or prawns while they were still swimming around in a tub and sit on crates, drinking beer whilst waiting for the food to be cooked. One evening there was a dog tied to a table. This was unusual, as dogs seemed to be quite rare. We made a fuss of it while we drank our beer. Then the chef came over and began shaving the dog's fur. I naively thought that he was doing it because of the extreme heat. I was wrong. With one swift movement of his hand he slit the dog's throat. Blood sprayed everywhere, running into the gutter under our feet. I thought I was going to be sick but the Chinese went about their business as if nothing had happened. We were so shocked at what had happened that we could not remain there and, shouting abuse at the bewildered chef, we stood up and left.

Most of our free evenings were spent drinking, often to the point where we were all legless. Because it was a naval base there were often visiting ships and, when they were in port, we always had a good time. The Dutch ships were the best. Their bars were open from the minute they docked, with beer at ten pence a bottle, and it was even permitted to smoke cannabis on board. We usually had very little time to take advantage of the situation, as the MPs would put the ships out of bounds to us the minute they discovered that there were drugs on board.

Whilst the Dutch were the most hospitable, the US Navy was the most spectacular. Their ships were bigger and better than any of the Royal Navy and if one of their aircraft carriers was in port there would be thousands of sailors wandering around the town. There was no love lost between the Royal Navy and the US Navy and fights often broke out, turning the streets into scenes more familiar in Western movies.

I was beginning to take an interest in sport again and decided that I had to lose some weight and get fit. I started to run and to work out in the gym. There was a tradition that the Forces would enter a team for the Dragon Boat races and I joined the combined Army and Navy women's team for the trials that were about to begin. Our PTI had great hopes for us.

The training for the trials was hard. The boats were long and low. Each woman had a paddle and the stroke was to the beat of a drum. It was much more difficult than I had imagined. After a practice lasting for only one hour my arms were aching and my hands were covered with blisters. The trials attracted a lot of overseas visitors, but, in spite of the competition, we made it through to the semi-final round where we were up against the Americans.

The race began with the American team jumping the gun. We had to paddle like mad to catch them and, at the finish, were neck and neck as we crossed the line. With their customary conceit, the Americans assumed they had won and began cheering and clapping. We just sat there, exhausted and down-hearted. Then the result was announced. 'The winner is . . . HMS *Tamar*! The American team is disqualified for a false start.'

We could hardly believe it. We were actually in the final of the Dragon Boat Race, to be held in Hong Kong harbour. The day of the final arrived and the weather was overcast. We sat in our boat as it bobbed about in the choppy water, waiting for the start. Next to us was a team from Japan. The gun sounded and the race began. Halfway down the course we began shipping water and knew that our chance of victory was over. The boat sank rapidly and we were left floundering in the water. Hong Kong may mean 'Fragrant Harbour' but it was awash with raw sewage. Within hours of being pulled out of the water, most of our team was in the sick bay suffering from acute stomach problems.

Later that evening there was a post-race party, held in one of the smart hotels. Despite the earlier fiasco some of us managed to attend and had a very good evening. We were all sportsmen and women, but the competitiveness we had felt during the race vanished in the atmosphere of the party. With a few drinks inside us, all our rivalry and cultural differences were forgotten.

When we made our way back to HMS *Tamar* we were in good spirits, laughing and giggling as we piled into the lift. It started to move upwards and suddenly a trip to the ladies became a priority. The lift stopped, the doors opened and we fell out and rushed into the ladies. Having used the facilities it occurred to me that I must be on the wrong floor because the toilet paper was soft. Only officers had soft toilet paper; lesser mortals had to use that hard stuff that was so useful to children for tracing but was totally ineffective for its real purpose. As we hung around by the lift waiting to go back to our own floor we all tried to keep quiet. The last thing we needed was to alert an officer to our genuine mistake. However, drunkenness and silence rarely go together and soon we were giggling helplessly once more. A door opened and there stood a new, teenage lieutenant, resplendent in a floral nightdress. She walked up to us and announced, 'You're all disgraceful. Report to me tomorrow morning; you're all on a charge.' At that moment the lift arrived and we fell into it and descended to our own floor.

The next morning Becky called me and told me that I had to be in my best uniform in fifteen minutes to see the Commanding Officer. Gradually the events of the previous evening started to come back to me. I wondered with which serious crime I would be charged: celebrating after a sporting event, using the wrong toilet, getting out of the lift on the wrong floor? I arrived at the Commanding Officer's door, was placed between two Gurkha NCOs and made to mark time. Each step played havoc with my hangover.

Eventually we marched into the office and I stood in front of the CO, staring straight ahead. He told me that my behaviour was unacceptable. It was a fair comment; we had been rather rowdy. I was quite willing to accept what he said until he continued by pointing out that rank was a privilege and that officers were selected for their superior qualities of leadership. Visions of a brainless, nineteen-year-old lieutenant, wearing a flowery nightie danced before my eyes. So, putting me on a charge for using the officers' toilet showed superior leadership qualities, did it? Once again the enormous gulf between those of us who had actually done something for our country and those who merely threw their weight around widened.

The CO finished his lecture by telling me that he was going to fine me thirty pounds. He asked if I had anything to say. 'Yes, Sir,' I replied, 'That's the most expensive penny I have ever spent!' He responded angrily, 'Forty pounds, Lance Corporal. Now get out!'

A few days later I was summoned to the office of Major T. I feared another bollocking for the toilet incident but she just said that she thought it was best forgotten. Then she handed me a letter and said, 'I think you might be interested in this. Congratulations, I knew you would do well.'

I quickly read the letter but could hardly believe what it said. I had been awarded a decoration. I stood there completely stunned while Major T pondered on the problem of how I could accept the award without blowing my cover. Both Becky and I had told everyone at HMS *Tamar* that we had been engaged on sensitive signal work and no one had ever challenged us. It was a good cover story up until that point, but to be awarded a decoration for that was not believable. I sat down and considered what to do. 'What does Becky say about her award?' I asked Major T. I naturally assumed that Becky would have been given the same award but I was wrong. There was nothing at all for her.

I left the office and went to find Becky. I was angry that she had been left out and it dampened the pleasure of my own award. Becky had worked so hard in Northern Ireland but her dedication had been ignored. I knew of total idiots who had been rewarded for doing absolutely nothing, not just MMs but QGMs as well. Of course there were those who deserved a medal, but others seemed to get them just for turning up. It occurred to me as I looked for Becky that perhaps it was because the Army was reluctant to admit that women were being used in front-line roles. At that time we were pioneers and the equality that seems to be creeping into the armed forces now was built on our work.

I found Becky in her room and told her of my award. I could

tell that she was disappointed but she congratulated me and we went for a drink to celebrate. Then I phoned home to tell my mother. I was disappointed with her reaction. When she answered the phone she sounded distant and distracted. I blurted out my news and she replied, 'Jackie, do you know what the time is?' I had to admit that I had no idea and she continued, 'It's four o'clock in the morning and I can't grasp what you are saying.' I apologized and promised to call her again at a more reasonable hour.

I began to receive letters from high-ranking officers congratulating me on my award. I am sure that they had no idea who I was; I certainly did not know who they were. The whole thing was ridiculous.

It was decided that the CO of the local regiment would present the award. He came into the commcen at the busiest time of the day and had to shout to make himself heard over the noise of the tape machines. At least he was honest enough to say that he did not have the foggiest idea what I had done to deserve it but that it was obviously not for being caught using the officers' lavs!

Another Christmas passed and Becky and I were beginning to be restless. It was boring to be stuck underground for fourteen hours at a stretch and the work itself was mind-numbing. We both decided that we would prefer to go back to Northern Ireland and so approached Major T to see if anything could be done. She made enquiries on our behalf and soon a secret signal arrived. The sergeant who received and decoded it thought that it was a joke and wanted to know how Becky and I had managed to break the secure network. We eventually convinced him that it was genuine and he handed it over to us. From the contents we knew that we could soon be on our way back to the United Kingdom.

The date chosen for our departure was the middle of April, which left barely a month to pack our belongings. In normal circumstances that would have been plenty of time but this was Hong Kong and I had no intention of leaving this shoppers' paradise without first pushing my credit card up to the limit!

Although the other girls were curious about the reasons for our three-year postings being cut short, they gave us a good send off.

It was wonderful finally to walk through the departure gate at Kai Tak airport, knowing that we were on our way home.

We settled into our seats and, after take off, consumed a few gin and tonics each. The flight was full of army personnel and their families and it was very noisy. A few hours after take-off I noticed that one of the crew kept walking up and down the aisle with a worried expression on his face. I thought no more about it until, soon after, an announcement was made by the captain informing us that they were having problems with the undercarriage and that we would be diverting into the nearest airport, which was Dubai.

As we came in to land at Dubai we all adopted the crash position. Although we had circled for a while and the control tower had confirmed that the undercarriage was down, we had no way of knowing whether or not it was actually locked. The atmosphere was tense as we made our approach but we landed safely and a huge cheer went up. Then we taxied off the far end of the runway and came to a stop miles away from the terminal building. The captain again made an announcement, this time to warn us that we could expect a hostile reception from the locals. He told us that American aircraft had bombed Libya and that Margaret Thatcher had openly supported the action. Now the Arab world was uniting in their condemnation of the Americans and their allies. He asked us to remain calm and not to create any problems with the authorities.

Shortly afterwards the local security forces surrounded the plane and armed police and soldiers came on board. They behaved badly, menacing women and children and waving their automatic weapons at the passengers, half frightening them to death. For eight hours we sat there, with neither food nor water. The heat was almost unbearable. Eventually some buses appeared and we were taken to the terminal building. As we drove away I turned to look at our plane and saw soldiers ransacking our luggage.

In the terminal we were made to walk in single file through a chanting mob. We were being pushed and shoved and it was only natural that some of the men reacted by trying to protect their families. They were kicked and punched for their troubles.

I suppose that the authorities thought that it would be safer to get rid of the British troublemakers and so the same coaches that had brought us to the building returned and we were made to get on board again. This time we drove for about an hour out into the desert. Becky and I were convinced that something nasty was about to happen to us and we both wished that we were armed. Never before in my life had I felt so out of control.

Our misgivings were unfounded, as we were taken to a huge hotel in the middle of nowhere. We disembarked and were ushered into the vast lobby where an airline representative was waiting for us. We were given a meal and shown to our rooms. Becky and I fared better than most of the families as we had managed to bring our hand baggage from the plane. I felt sorry for some of the passengers who were trying to cope with babies and small children without clean clothes or even nappies. The airline staff tried to help us, but there was little that they could do. For twenty-four hours we were virtual prisoners in the hotel. Then the buses turned up once more and took us back to the airport where we boarded the plane. After a short time we taxied out to the runway and began our take-off run. Soon the aircraft became airborne and we climbed and turned, heading for home.

As we were approaching British air space, the captain told us that there was fog at Gatwick airport and that we might have to divert to Manchester. After all that we had been through since leaving Hong Kong, this was the final straw. I thought that there might be a riot among the passengers but at the last minute the fog cleared sufficiently for us to land.

Mum was waiting at the airport and was overjoyed to see me. She had spent a fortune hiring a taxi to bring me home. I had two relaxing weeks with her, catching up with family life again before I met up with Becky once more and we made our way to Camp Alpha for yet another training course.

CHAPTER SIXTEEN

I arrived overweight, out of condition and in need of some serious training. I spent a week catching up with news from the instructors and familiarizing myself with the weapons again. I was promoted to Corporal and at the end of that week I was given another identity card and a Northern Ireland driving licence, this time in the name of Jackie Snowdon.

In the twelve months that I had been away a lot had changed. The Intelligence Corps was trying to get overall control of 14 Company and some of the lads used this as a means of staying in Northern Ireland. After their tour was complete they were allowed to leave their regiments and join the Intelligence Corps with the promise that they could stay in Northern Ireland or take a posting where they could work against the communist bloc countries. Freddie, Hugh and Danny had all chosen this route.

I heard that the Det had been falling into bad habits and Becky and I came back to an atmosphere of open hostility. Steve had gone and the new boss was a weak-willed individual who informed us that we would have problems working again, as no one wanted a woman for a partner. He later admitted that two of the lads had, in fact, offered to work with us but he was of the opinion that they were not very enthusiastic about it. One was an old timer, Roy, who was on his third tour in the province; the other was Keith, a completely new op on his first tour. The only thing that had improved since I had left was that the rules about women living outside of the complex had been relaxed and Becky and I were allocated a basha on the base.

Keith and I teamed up and immediately began to clash.

Although he was a new op and had had no experience at all he thought he was entitled to lay down ground rules and he gave me a lecture on how he expected me to behave. We had words about his attitude and I pointed out that he was the one who was new to the job, not me. It made no difference to him; he seemed to think that it was my duty to obey him. We argued constantly and one morning Keith announced that he had been to the boss and told him that he would not work with me any more. Once again I was without a partner and therefore unable to work.

I went up to see the boss myself. He sat, head down, and refused to look me in the eye. Rick, who had been my first partner, was now back again as the acting operations officer. He took me to one side and said, 'Look, Jackie, you can't work on your own and no one wants a partner. They think it's a sign of weakness.' Before he had the chance to say anything more he was interrupted.

Dave, a quiet chap who had been around during my first tour, suddenly announced, 'I'd like a partner.'

So Dave, whom the others had ridiculed for his obsession with weightlifting, became my knight in shining armour. We went to his basha and sat down to discuss how we would work together.

Dave was honest enough to admit that he sometimes struggled with surveillance and that driving, map reading and talking on the radio all at the same time was impossible. I knew what he meant and wondered how others like Keith could be so arrogant as to think that they could manage to do all of that by themselves. It was bad enough during the day but at night time the only way to read a map was to perch it on your knee and look at it by the light of a pencil torch, gripped in your teeth. That alone made driving difficult and talking on the radio impossible. It was a proven fact that teams of two people did the major part of the work and that single ops were nowhere near as good. Despite this the Army allowed ops to work on their own, as long as they were males of course. The same Army that banned women from manning OPs in case they needed to spend a penny allowed men to work alone even though they were far less effective. The Army cared nothing for the feelings of the women ops but would happily compromise operations rather than dent the egos of these arrogant young men.

Dave and I soon became a very effective team. I saw very little of Becky as she and Roy were on opposite shifts to us in order to keep the double-crewed cars out for most of the time.

We received information that a huge bomb had been placed under the road near to the border with the Republic. On the basis of this information they sent a team to Fermanagh and, sure enough, the command wire to the bomb was found. The team set up an ambush.

Late one night two IRA men arrived, armed with automatic rifles. A firefight ensued, leaving one man dead and the other wounded. Everyone was pleased with the success of the operation. It was obvious that the bomb had been intended to blow up a police or an army patrol. What made it so good from our point of view was that the information about the bomb had come from Army sources and not from the Police. Usually everything was channelled through the Police who then decided which leads were worth pursuing.

Life at work was becoming considerably better than it had been when I returned to Northern Ireland and it was not just work that had improved. My private life had taken an upturn as well, in the form of a Sergeant named Peter. He was in charge of the Support Unit and lived in the basha directly opposite to where Becky and I lived. He was tall and slim and had a wonderful personality. In a very short time I found myself falling in love with him and he seemed to feel the same about me.

The majority of our work centred on Location F and Location B and the ops began to appreciate the role that the double-crewed cars played. Time after time the single cars were compromised. A man sitting alone in a parked car in the middle of a housing estate soon attracted unwanted attention. The single ops were forever changing both their cars and their hairstyles, but Dave and I had no such problems. Soon morons like Keith were in the minority and those who had shown contempt for us at the start were admitting that they had been wrong.

On several occasions the locations of weapons hides were identified. We set up observation posts near these weapons hides so we could follow the cars when they were likely to be carrying weapons.

When cars visited these sites the observation post would alert control. The helicopter would usually arrive first and the ground teams would have to cruise around looking for the suspect car. It was never known if the terrorists in the cars were about to use the weapons they had just picked up.

During one such operation Dave and I were following a blue Fiesta, when there was a screech of brakes in front of us. Dave stopped the car and we both looked at the Fiesta which had done a U turn. I stared at the target who was angrily waving at us to move out of his way. Dave pulled over and smiled at him and he sped off down the road. Fortunately the helicopter was able to pick up the surveillance and the pilot managed to identify the house to which the car had been driven.

The boss told Dave and me to do a drive past to see what was happening at the house. We drove into the village and immediately realized that our car had been compromised. There were lookouts or 'dickers' all over the place, checking to see if anyone had followed the target. We drove straight through the village and out the other side before reporting back to the base. The boss wanted us to drive past again to see if there had been any change. The man was a complete idiot. If we showed our faces again the terrorists were likely to spring an illegal vehicle checkpoint which would, inevitably, end in a gunfight. We refused to do as he had asked and drove back to camp.

At the debriefing the boss was furious with us for disobeying his orders and gave us a good bollocking. I began to wonder how on earth a dickhead like him had ever got through the selection process. Rick decided to step in on Dave's and my behalf and took the boss to one side and explained why we had refused to obey his orders. Thanks to Rick we were exonerated.

The boss had no understanding of the difficulties that ops faced on the street day after day. In a way this was not entirely his fault as he had come over to Ireland as a new op but had been put in command almost immediately. He had gained no first-hand experience of what we had to go through but it required very little imagination to know that the more we paraded ourselves in front of groups of terrorists the more likely it was that we would find ourselves in serious trouble.

More ops began to arrive from England. Some were new to Northern Ireland, while others were on their second or even third tour. Ross was back for a second time and was still barking mad. He found a soul mate in one of the new boys, a great bear of a man called Jerry. He was one of those larger than life characters who caused havoc wherever he went, but he had a great sense of humour.

Whenever Jerry was on bar duty he always got as drunk as the people he was serving and it was on one of these occasions that he became convinced there was a rat behind the bar. He was the only one who ever heard the rat scrabbling around among the bags of crisps. He would stop what he was doing and make us all listen for the sound of the little rodent but no one else ever heard a thing.

One evening, after more ranting about vermin, he disappeared from the bar to return moments later with a Remington Repeater shotgun. 'I'll show that bloody rat who the boss is round here,' he yelled, advancing towards the bar. We backed away. By now the room was silent and Jerry was listening for evidence that Ratty was on the move. 'Hear that?' he whispered.

I strained my ears but all I heard was more silence, which was shattered seconds later by the sound of Jerry's shotgun. He began blasting away at the boxes of crisps and snacks behind the bar and we all took cover to avoid being hit by peanut shrapnel. Eventually the shooting stopped and Jerry said with satisfaction, 'That's got the bastard.' He began sifting through the debris behind the bar, looking for the body, but as we expected he found nothing. 'Bugger,' he said, 'I must have winged him.'

He walked out. Several of the SAS lads who had been in their basha next door had come storming into the bar and now formed an armed circle around it. Jerry passed through the circle and went out into the night muttering 'Rats!' The boss tried to give him a bollocking but his words passed right over Jerry's head. He was convinced he was right. Somewhere behind the bar was a rat;

wounded, of course, but still waiting to create a mess with the crisps.

During my first tour the RUC surveillance team had stayed within the Belfast area, working mainly with the East Det. I was surprised when Rick announced one day that they were running an operation in our area and that we would be needed for back-up. Our briefing room was packed on the day of the operation. The RUC team told us that a dustcart was being driven out of the city. They had a team following it, as they believed that it would be packed with explosives and would then return to Belfast. We were again told that this was a police job and that we were only there for back-up. They stressed that it was their show and that they wanted no interference from us.

It was a hot day and Dave and I enjoyed a leisurely drive along the main road. We parked in a lay-by and had an ice cream. Rick was relaying news of the van's progress to us over our net, since the Police were not keen for us to share a radio channel. The follow was going well. The van had pulled off the main road and was followed by a couple of Det cars to a farm. After a while it pulled out of the yard and started back along the road to the city. Before long it made another detour as the driver pulled off the road into a pub car park. He got down from his cab and went into the pub. Two of the police surveillance team went in after him and reported that the driver had met a contact and that they were both sitting in the pub restaurant eating their lunch. This was one occasion where the police surveillance team fared better than we would have done. Being Irish, they could go into pubs and restaurants without arousing suspicion. Had we done the same we would have been instantly recognized by our accents. Time dragged by as we sat in the sweltering heat in our car. The radio was silent; obviously the driver and his contact were having a leisurely lunch

Suddenly Dave asked, 'What was the reg of that van, again?' I told him, but asked why he was checking. 'Because it's just passed us,' he replied. Flinging the remains of our ice creams out of the window we began to follow the dustcart as it lumbered up a hill. As we came closer and looked at the numberplate we could see that there was no mistake; this was the target van.

I got straight on the radio, 'Zero from Tango. We have X One mobile towards Blue One Two.' Rick's puzzled voice came back immediately, 'Tango, are you sure?' The van was picking up speed as I confirmed that it was the target van that we were following. There was a long pause and then I heard Rick say, 'Tango, you're on your own. Target has been lost. Stick with it.' What had begun as an easy afternoon was rapidly turning into a nightmare. We estimated that we were at least eight miles from where the RUC team thought the driver was having his lunch. Over the radio I could hear the rest of the Det shouting that they were trying to catch up with us. We did not even have the benefit of the helicopter. It was out of action that day. On the motorway we dropped back slightly and went past our normal cut-off point. The dustcart was heading for the city and we had no maps of the area. Our team and the RUC police surveillance team were still miles behind us.

When the van came off the motorway we knew that we would have to follow it right into the city. Neither Dave nor I knew where we were and had to constantly relay our position to Rick, who insisted that we stick with the van. By now it had entered a Nationalist area. It was like another world; tricolours adorned the lampposts and there were huge murals depicting IRA heroes on the sides of the buildings. The van pulled off on to a side street and stopped. Dave pulled up outside a corner shop and switched off the engine. We got out of the car and, hand in hand, walked past the van. On the corner stood two young men. They were obviously the lookouts (dickers) and were taking a great interest in us. Dave nodded to them and we casually crossed the road. Glancing to my right I could see the driver of the van talking animatedly to another man. We walked further on and stopped in an alleyway, holding each other in a clinch. We were both aware that our personal radios did not work in this area and that we had no backup. It was difficult to know what to do. Rick had insisted that we follow the van and keep it in sight to allow time for the others to catch up but we were now dangerously close to being caught ourselves. I leaned towards Dave and whispered in his ear, 'We've got to get back to the car.' He nodded his agreement and, in as relaxed a manner as we could, we sauntered back towards the car. I could feel the eyes of the dickers on us all the time and I knew that if they were to challenge us the game would be up. The minute we opened our mouths they would know that we were British.

After a tense few moments we reached the car and got in. I called up Rick and he told me that the RUC team was in the area and that Dave and I could back off and leave it to them. Gratefully we drove off, trying to remember the way out of the back streets. Eventually we found a route that we recognized and started back towards our base.

We arrived back at camp after everyone else. The Head of Special Branch with LB and the RUC team boss were already there and were standing talking to Rick. How could things have gone so badly wrong? In the safety of our own surroundings I gave way to the anger that had been building inside me and shouted at the Police, 'How the hell could you miss a bloody dustcart moving off from the restaurant? I thought you had two ops in there keeping tabs on the driver.' They looked uncomfortable, but could give me no answer. It was unbelievable. The van must have been missing for at least fifteen minutes when it passed Dave and me, and yet, if we had not alerted them, they would never have known that it had gone. Jerry asked them bluntly, 'Whose bloody side are you lot on?' and a blazing row ensued with both sides shouting and pointing fingers at the other.

The next day we were annoyed to hear on the news that, 'Following a successful Police operation yesterday, a large quantity of explosives has been recovered.'

CHAPTER SEVENTEEN

Dave and I worked very well together and I enjoyed being his partner. He was an absolute gentleman who treated me with respect and who never needed to belittle anyone to make himself feel superior. Unfortunately it was this harmony that led to the break-up of our partnership. A new boss had arrived, also called Dave. He decided that the new ops were not as effective as they could be and that they needed a bit of 'nursing' from some of the old hands. In the six months that we had been back Becky and I had become well-respected ops and the boss decided that Becky should partner a new chap called Grant, while I would partner Rod.

It was sad that my partnership with Dave had to end, but, on a personal level, my relationship with Peter was progressing very well. We were both sure that it was serious and were very happy until the Army spoilt it for us by posting Peter to Belize. They could not have found a more remote place if they had tried and we were devastated by the news, knowing that we would not be able to see each other for at least six months. Peter went off to his jungle-covered, spider-infested outpost in Central America and I moped around in a warehouse in Northern Ireland. It was not a happy time for either of us.

One day I was called into the boss's office and told that another unit had asked for me to do an undercover operation with one of their men, Neil. I went over to their block to see what it was all about. Their boss told me that there was a holiday house situated in a large seaside town along the east coast. It belonged to a well-known personality and information had been received that an explosive device was going to be planted in the house. The plan was for Neil and me to act as newly weds and to book into a hotel just opposite the back of the house. From our bedroom we would be able to watch the house and at the same time some of the lads from the unit would be hidden on a boat, to cover the front of the property.

Fortunately for us this seaside town was in a mainly Protestant area and so English visitors were not unusual. We booked in and Neil soon charmed the hotel staff with his wit and crazy sense of humour. We had packed our bags with radios, guns and ammunition, leaving very little room for clothes. However, since we were pretending to be newly married, we had no plans to go out much and so would be able to survive without a change of clothes.

Our bedroom was perfectly placed. We could see both the boat bobbing up and down and the back of the property from the window and decided to operate a two-hour roster for keeping watch. The first night passed quietly. We watched the other lads board the boat and disappear below. Two hours later one of them was hanging over the side, throwing up. Obviously the bobbing about was not to his liking!

In the morning we had to pack everything into our bags so that we could go down to breakfast and give the maid a chance to make up our room. In the dining room we sat holding hands and gazing lovingly into each other's eyes across the table. We finished eating, but knew that we had not allowed enough time for the maid to sort out the room, so we decided to go for a stroll along the front. We had gone about a quarter of a mile when Neil suddenly exclaimed, 'Shit! Me pistol's under the pillow!' We made a frantic dash back to the hotel and burst into the reception area startling the girl behind the desk. Neil shouted to her, 'She can't keep 'er hands off me, luv,' as we rushed to our room. I grabbed the pillow from the bed and there was the pistol. Seconds later as we sat on the bed trying to get our breath back, the door opened and the maid walked in. Neil beamed at her and said, 'Give us another half hour, will ya, luv.' She blushed and scuttled out of the room. We spent four days in the hotel and saw nothing. No one even approached the house and the Police lost interest in it.

Arriving back at the Det I found that the action was again centred in the city area. We had information that a man known to be a cold, calculating killer was forming a new ASU. Special Branch decided that we should carry out a raid on his house while he was away to see if we could gain any information.

We carried out a number of recces, always with the back-up of the HMSU of the RUC and sometimes with the Army on the ground.

The night came when the raid was to take place. Craig and I were detailed to drop off eight Special Army ops in our transit van prior to the others going in on the ground. The village where the house was situated was surrounded by moorland and that night there was a layer of mist swirling just above the ground. The effect was really eerie. As we drove towards the drop-off point I could hear the Army lads in the back of the van getting ready. Then, in the rear-view mirror, I saw the headlights of a car coming towards us. I told Craig, but he had already seen the lights, so I called control on the radio and told them that we would go round again to lose the other vehicle. I was just about to tell the lads in the back what was happening when the van lurched forward. I could hear bodies falling over and somebody shouted, 'Jesus, he's rammed us!' Craig fought to control the van but we were hit again. The guys in the back were getting very agitated and wanted to know what was going on. I called up Rick at control and told him that we were having problems. He advised us that the HMSU was travelling towards a junction up ahead of us and would set up a police roadblock. Craig shook his head but drove on. The car behind was weaving backwards and forwards, but, since it was a narrow road, was unable to pass us. He hit us once more as we came around a corner. Up in front of us we saw the roadblock already in place with a car across the road. 'Right, that's it,' Craig sighed with relief and pulled over, switching off the engine. He and I leapt out of the van, our HK53s at the ready. We raced round to the back and saw that the car had also stopped and was half in the ditch; the driver was slumped across the steering wheel. Levelling our weapons, we approached the car. Behind us the van door slid open and out tumbled eight very angry Army soldiers.

Between us we surrounded the car. The driver was motionless. Then the police took over. Cautiously they opened the car door. One of them bent over and put his head into the car. He stood up and announced, 'He's drunk as a skunk!' The driver was semi-conscious and mumbling about 'just one more drink' as they pulled him from the car. We all stood about in the country lane, in the dark, feeling very silly. Then someone suggested that we get back to work and so we all piled back into the van and went round one more time to make sure we were not being followed. Then we dropped the Army team and the entire operation went like clockwork from that moment.

Later the Police called to give us the full story on the drunken driver. Apparently he had been at a party and had drunk too much. When he left the party to drive home he had seen the lights on our van and thought they were those of a friend who lived nearby. He therefore decided to keep close to the friend and so latched on to our tail lights. He said that he kept falling asleep and only woke up when he felt a bump. He didn't seem to realize that he had caused the bump by driving into the back of our van and could remember nothing more about the entire evening!

The information that was gathered from the raid provided us with very interesting intelligence. Special Branch discovered that an off-duty soldier was being targeted by the IRA. He regularly used a fish and chip shop on the same day and time each week. He was the perfect target for the terrorists. We did not know where the IRA group was based, which was a worry for us as they were totally out of our control. What we did know was that they had access to Armalite rifles. It was decided that the Army would shadow the man to the fish and chip shop on the day that Special Branch thought the job would be going down. Tony, the sergeant who was in charge, decided that the best way to maintain cover was for Becky and me to be involved. The Det had moved to save travelling time and we were based at another Army camp. We lived in portakabins that were kept well away from the other troops who were based there. Astonishingly, the Police decided that the off-duty soldier did not need to know that he was a potential target. Even now I still find it unbelievable that they took that decision.

Tony and I ran a circuit around the fish and chip shop checking the hedgerows for any signs of an IRA ambush. I was dressed in a tracksuit with my pistol strapped tightly to my waist and a radio rubbing against my bare skin. I was also carrying a small haversack on my back that contained an MP5K. Becky and her partner were on standby to take over from us after a couple of hours.

After running around for a couple of miles dressed like this, I was beginning to work up quite a sweat. Then the off-duty soldier arrived in his car and Tony and I walked across the car park towards him. He looked up and smiled and made his way over to the shop. We followed closely behind him. I took the haversack off my back and kept it in my hand ready to grab the machine pistol inside. The soldier was totally oblivious to what was going on and stopped to chat to a young woman. He had stopped in a wide open space where there was no cover of any kind and Tony and I had no choice but to walk past him and loiter around the entrance. Suddenly my earpiece began to buzz and the message came through that one of the IRA cars had been seen approaching the chip shop with three men on board. This was ridiculous. The soldier was totally ignorant of the fact that he was about to be shot dead and stood there completely unprotected, chatting casually to a civilian who presumably would also share his fate. Tony made a snap decision. Sprinting towards the soldier, he grabbed him by the shoulder and dragged him into the entrance, pushing him into an alcove. He towered over the stunned man and hissed at him, 'Shut up. I'm doing you a big favour here.' The soldier must have sensed that he had no reason to be frightened of Tony and he nodded.

As casually as we could Tony and I stood in front of the man, hiding him from view. We avoided looking at the girl behind the counter who was obviously wondering what was happening. The IRA vehicle drove slowly past the car park. Behind came an army car with four soldiers on board. The terrorists were not stupid. When they saw the car approaching them from the rear they must have realized that we were waiting for them and they sped off, leaving the soldier unharmed. If the soldier had been told that he was a potential target it would have been so much easier to protect him and possibly apprehend the terrorists as well. Since he had not been told, he not only put himself in danger but also, unwittingly, endangered the lives of innocent civilians in the area. In spite of the soldier being unharmed, Special Branch was furious with Tony and me for intervening. They thought that we should have allowed the job to happen, regardless of the outcome. Later on they very grudgingly agreed to inform the soldier that he had been a target. I never did find out what his reaction was to the news. I suspect that he, like us, wondered just whose side the Police were on.

Summer passed and in late October the Police suddenly decided that we were ready for a move. We were transferred to cover an operation in Location F. LB attended our briefing and told us that there was an ASU active there and that they were planning to travel to Location A that night to pick up some weapons. We knew the target and so the boss detailed Liam, Ross, Jerry, Damian, Rod and me to follow him. We took three cars, which was more than enough for the job. Rod and I sat in a lay-by and watched as the target car drove past. Sure enough the driver was the terrorist that we all knew. With him he had three other men. We tailed him all the way to Location A where he parked in front of a known Republican bar. It was nine o'clock and the town was quiet. Rod and I parked in the wide market place close to where Jerry had left his car. Ross strolled over and leaned against our car commenting, 'This is a doddle.' He then ambled back towards his car and, as he reached it the road behind us erupted with the sound of automatic fire. We were being fired at by the terrorists, but in the chaos and noise of the scene we were unable to see from where they were attacking us. Rod threw our car into reverse and we hurtled out of the market place with Ross's car roaring past us. The radio net was alive with noise as all the ops escaped from the town.

Rod and I drove about half a mile outside the town and then parked to try to catch our breath and find out what had happened to the others. We had just heard that everyone was safe when from behind came the sound of an engine and some headlights appeared, blinding us temporarily. The vehicle screeched to a halt and some men got out and began walking towards us. This time Rod and I were ready for them. As they approached an Irish voice shouted out to us, 'You in the car, get out!' We were both clutching our MP5Ks as a figure appeared at the window and levelled a SLR at Rod. I could hardly believe what I was seeing. This was no terrorist but a soldier from the Ulster Defence Regiment. Once again our own side was targeting us. Other soldiers had made a ring around the car. They were obviously reacting to the shooting in town. I wound down my window and found myself staring down the barrel of a SLR. I was angry by now and said to the soldier holding the gun, 'Get that thing out of my face and I will get out of the car. I'm a member of the Security Forces.' The soldier backed away. At that moment Jerry and Ross arrived and shouted at the soldiers to back off. It was an uneasy stand-off. Rod and I slowly got out of our car, holding our weapons at our sides. We faced the soldiers who looked much more frightened than we felt. Then the HMSU arrived and calmed the situation.

It was a tremendous relief to arrive back at the Det. We sat in the briefing room joking among ourselves while we waited for the debriefing to begin. The Head of Special Branch marched in accompanied by LB. This was unusual but we soon found out why he was there. Puffing on a cigarette he calmly told us that we had been set up. He told us that the RUC knew that the ASU were out to trap some soldiers and they allowed it to happen in order to identify the IRA terrorists.

Rod blurted out, 'But you almost got us all killed.' The Head looked at Rod, a patronising smirk on his face, and replied, 'In this game, son, you're all acceptable casualties.' With that he swept from the room.

Jerry yelled, 'Bastard!' after him but he had gone. We were in shock at what he had told us. He was no better than the terrorists he was supposed to be fighting; for him life was cheap as long as it was not his life. Jerry suddenly turned to Ross and me and said, 'Come on, I've got a plan.'

We followed him into the romper room, where we sat down to work out the details. Then Rod went down to the bar to check that the Head and LB were both having a drink. He came back and confirmed that the coast was clear. Their car, a large Granada with bullet-proof windows, was parked outside the operations block. While I kept watch, Jerry and Ross slid underneath it and attached couple of flashbangs to the underside. They crawled back out with huge grins on their faces. We went into the bar as if nothing had happened.

After drinking vast quantities of our beer, the Head of Special Branch decided it was time to go home. His driver led the way out to the car. By now most of the Det knew that something was going on and had begun to gather outside. As the car swept into the compound he waved to us. Suddenly the car erupted in a ball of flames and smoke. It swerved to a halt and the driver baled out. I heard Dave, the boss, mutter, 'Oh, bugger!' and then two of the ops ran over to the car to see the Head's reaction to our little joke. They quickly returned, shaking with laughter. 'He's shit himself,' one of them reported when he stopped laughing. We felt very pleased with ourselves and thought that justice had been done.

The following day Jerry, Ross and I were summoned to Dave's office. He was very matter of fact about the whole thing. He told us that the Head had made a complaint against us and that we would all have to carry the can for our moment of fun. Despite the fact that he had nearly got us killed he actually had the nerve to complain about our prank. It cost us a barrel of beer and a fine of twenty pounds each. The worst thing was that Ross and I were due for promotion but that was put on hold. It had also been decided that Jerry and I should have a break from operations.

The Army's idea of giving us a break was to send us on a parachute course. Neither of us had ever made a parachute jump before. The first day we practised jumping off chairs and learning how to fall correctly. Later that afternoon, as the weather was good, the instructor decided it was time for us to jump. The three of us squashed into a tiny aeroplane and took off. That part was good, just like being in the helicopter. Then the instructor hooked me up to the static line and nodded. I looked out of the open door and suddenly thought that this was not a practice, it was the real thing. The hardest thing I have ever done in my life was to launch myself through that open door, praying to God that the parachute would open. As I fell I could feel my stomach tightening and then I was jerked upwards as the parachute opened. Suddenly it was the best feeling in the world, floating gently down towards the green fields. I was amazed at how quiet it was. Then the ground seemed to rush towards me and I prepared for the landing; knees together, hit the ground and roll. As I landed the wind caught my parachute and I was pulled along the ground. I managed to stop, bundled the chute into my arms and walked back to the hangar. Although I had not looked forward to the course and the thought of leaping from an aeroplane had filled me with dread, the experience was wonderful.

Unfortunately the weather was deteriorating and we knew that we would not be able to stay for much longer. Before it closed in completely Jerry and I managed to do five more jumps. Then, reluctantly, we had to return to the Det.

CHAPTER EIGHTEEN

Things were becoming hectic once more and soon all thoughts of parachuting were behind me as I immersed myself in my work. Special Branch had received information that an Active Service Unit was planning a spectacular.

We had identified some of the ASU members and knew that they were hard men, devoted to the IRA cause. If we allowed them to, they were capable of causing a great deal of trouble.

By May, 1987, we believed the spectacular was to be an attack on the Loughall police station and everyone in it. It would be similar to a stunt they had pulled off the previous year when the same unit had successfully destroyed the Birches RUC station. We knew that it was possible that the operation would succeed, as the ASU was a skilled and highly professional unit. We had the heavy responsibility of stopping it. The SAS were brought in for this purpose. This was by far the biggest operation I had ever seen.

However, we still lacked details. The RUC officers who normally manned Loughall police station were taken out and replaced by members of the SAS dressed in the green uniforms of the RUC. South Det and E4A, Special Branch's own surveillance specialists mounted surveillance operations over an extended period to try to gather information. HMSU was deployed to set up road blocks and ops from Det were spread across a wide area and were tasked with picking up the terrorists as they arrived for the spectacular.

As the days went by tension increased and the pressure on us to pick up the members of the ASU was enormous. Hour after hour we sat watching road junctions and chasing possible suspects, but to no avail. By five pm on that Friday I was convinced that we had blown it. What I did not know then was that late that afternoon the terrorists had hijacked a blue Toyota van from the Dungannon area. They had also stolen a mechanical digger, which they parked in a farmyard belonging to a Republican sympathizer. The huge bomb, with which they intended to destroy the police station, was placed in the front bucket of the digger and the terrorists armed themselves with Armalites and G3 automatic rifles. There were eight terrorists in the unit.

As the blue van made its way along the winding country lanes into the village of Loughall it was spotted by an op from the Det. Rod and I saw it as it passed us at a junction and we began following it as best we could. It was not easy in the confines of the narrow lanes and it was made worse by the digger, which was lumbering along close on the tail of the van. We followed it right into the village and then we and all the other ops from the Det pulled back and the SAS took over. Behind them vehicles from the Det and the HMSU blocked every route out of Loughall. Then we waited.

The SAS were watching the police station and saw the digger stop outside and park against the wall. The terrorists got out of the van and levelled their weapons at the police station. A second or two passed and then the firing began. The bomb exploded, showering the area with debris. The police station was badly damaged and some of the SAS team inside were injured, although not fatally.

Sadly one man, a civilian, was caught in the crossfire and was killed. The noise was incredible. Rod and I were sitting in our car less than a mile away and the bomb explosion made us jump. We waited in the car, not knowing how successful the operation had been until we heard the boss calling over the radio for us all to return to base. As we moved off Puma and Gazelle helicopters moved in to the village to take out the SAS teams.

We reached base after the SAS lads and found them in jubilant mood. They were like small children, excitedly re-enacting the parts they had played that afternoon. Then it was confirmed that all eight terrorists had been killed and a great cheer went up. Later that evening in the bar the talk was of nothing else. Over and over the events were described, each op claiming to have killed at least one terrorist.

The party mood lasted for days; it seemed that the SAS could do no wrong. The media gave the operation huge coverage and the headlines in one of the tabloids next day said simply 'Eight – Nil'.

Our work continued, but at a more mundane level. I had no doubt that there would never be another operation like Loughall and that it would take a very long time for the IRA to recover from such a resounding defeat. For myself I sincerely hoped that I would not have to go through such a stressful time again.

In November the IRA planted a bomb in a disused school building in Enniskillen. When it exploded, it killed eleven people and injured a further sixty-three as part of the building collapsed. It seemed all the more tragic as the people had been gathering for the annual Remembrance Day ceremony.

I began to think seriously about my job. Not only did I feel disgust at the callousness of the IRA, I was also becoming more and more disillusioned with the way situations were manipulated by the very people who should have been upholding the law. When I had joined the Det I had been a naïve twenty-year-old. I really believed that I could make a difference with the work I would be doing. I would help to get rid of the IRA and Northern Ireland would become a safe and peaceful place in which to live.

What a joke! There could never be peace while certain groups manipulated the situation to suit themselves. The IRA and other Catholic groups believed that by killing Protestants they could have a united Ireland. The Protestants believed that by killing Catholics they could remain part of Britain and not have to unite with the rest of Ireland. The Police, who had jurisdiction over the Army, seemed to believe they could do whatever they wanted and get away with it. The sad truth was that they probably could. They were not concerned with people dying; they could even arrange for you to die if it suited their purpose. Although there were many good people who wanted peace more than anything, the whole situation in that troubled land was controlled by psychopaths who enjoyed killing for its own sake. I knew that thoughts like this meant only one thing; my love affair with the Det was over and it was time for me to leave Ireland.

I knew that it would be impossible to return to the Royal Signals after this tour. My entire attitude to the Army had changed. The sex discrimination and petty rules and regulations suddenly seemed completely pointless to me. I was no longer keen to stand to attention and salute a brainless teenager whose sole qualification for becoming an officer was the plum in her mouth. After everything I had lived through, that side of the Army held no attraction for me whatsoever.

I decided, like many of my friends, that my best course of action would be to join the Intelligence Corps. A number of former ops had gone over to the Int Corps to receive their new cap badge. It was as simple as that. They were not required to retrain, they only had to go through a few background notes and they became part of the Int Corps. They were then used for training or operational purposes either back in Ireland or over in Germany. Of course the men had the option of joining the SAS. That was a choice not open to women at that time. Although women were good enough to be attached to the SAS and had performed many valuable roles for them, they were not considered suitable to join the Regiment.

I spoke to the bosses at HQ in Lisburn and told them that I wanted to relocate to the Intelligence Corps. A few phone calls were made and I assumed that the rest would be a mere formality. Then I received a letter from the training department at WRAC HQ in Guildford. They had decided that, before I could relocate, I had to be reassessed for suitability. I again checked with the bosses in Lisburn but they told me not to worry; the reassessment was a formality. They gave me an air ticket and off I went.

I arrived back in Guildford eight years after I had finished my basic training there. Nothing much had changed. I walked into the Education block wearing my best skirt and blouse. My hair was down to my shoulders. An officious female Corporal greeted me with the words, 'Where is your uniform?'

I explained that I no longer wore a uniform. She looked at me as if I was totally mad and told me that I could not see the Captain as I was improperly dressed. I again explained to her that I was with a unit that did not wear uniform, in fact I no longer possessed a uniform. The Corporal obviously thought I was lying and, after giving me a long, hard stare, she flounced out of the room, to return some moments later with a bundle of papers. She told me to sit down at a desk and turn over the paper that had been placed on it. It was a list of instructions for completing a test paper. She then began to read the list to me, droning on until I politely told her that I would prefer to read it myself. She paused, her face scarlet, and angrily told me that she always read out the instructions. So much for the reassessment being a formality! I was being treated like a raw recruit who was not too bright. If she had been a little more pleasant I might have felt sorry for the Corporal. Obviously reading out the instructions had been the high point of her day and I had spoiled it for her!

The test paper itself was ridiculously easy. There was a section covering basic arithmetic and another for basic English. The last section required a brief description of the job I was already doing. I completed the first two parts but left the page blank for the last question. Having finished the test I stood up and took my paper over to the Corporal. She immediately wanted to know who had told me I could move. 'I did,' I muttered, 'and here are my completed papers, thank you.' I handed her my test papers and she stalked out of the room, a pained expression on her face.

Within minutes I was called into the Captain's office and told where to stand. She was sitting at her desk, studying my test papers. Eventually she looked up and enquired, 'What gives you the right to question my staff, Corporal?'

She then told me to sit down and asked why I had not completed the last section of the test. I told her that I was bound by the Official Secrets Act and that I was not at liberty to discuss my work with anyone. She raised her eyebrows and, with a sneer, called me a liar. I suppose that, for a pen pusher, this sort of secrecy was a concept that she found hard to comprehend. She demanded to know the name of my Officer in Command. I told her and added, 'He works in Lisburn, Ma'am.'

She picked up her phone and asked to be put through to him. She introduced herself and stated the reason for her call. She obviously expected confirmation that I was lying to her, but as she listened her face tightened. She hung up, barely able to hide her fury and hissed at me, 'I don't know what's so special about you.' Then she added in a voice full of spite, 'I am not recommending you for transfer.' I looked at her and said, 'With respect, Ma'am, if you telephone the Int Corps I think you will find that it has already been approved.'

She told me to get out of her office and wait outside. She kept me waiting outside the office for over an hour and then called me back in. She was so angry that she could hardly speak to me in a civil manner. 'It seems that you know people in high places, Corporal George,' she said. 'You are expected in January. It appears that there was nothing I could do about it. Now get out!'

As I left the camp I knew that I could not stand this attitude for much longer. I was heartily sick of the 'them' and 'us' syndrome and of having to defer to officers who did not seem to think it necessary to be polite to those of lower rank. I had absolutely no doubt that I was much more capable than the nasty Captain I had just encountered and I wondered if she had ever done anything useful. I had a suspicion that she was one of those people who misunderstood the meaning of the words assertion and aggression and thought that they were the same thing. She probably spent her whole life sitting behind a desk talking down to people.

Since I was not expected until January I went back to the Det and began packing up my belongings. Everything I had fitted into an Escort van that had been compromised and was being returned to the mainland. When I was ready I said goodbye to my colleagues and left the Det for the last time. I took a ferry to Stranraer and drove home from there.

Mum was waiting for me and hugged me as I walked through the door. She knew that I had finished with Northern Ireland and

I could see the look of relief on her face. The time I had spent over the water had taken a toll on Mum too and, although I knew she would never have tried to stop me doing anything I wanted, she was certainly pleased to have me home in one piece. We spent a few days together and then I made my way down to the Templer Barracks, training depot of the Intelligence Corps.

I was issued with a complete new uniform and told that I would be sleeping in a four-bed room. I was staggered. One of the very few perks of the job for an NCO was a single room but I was expected to share a room with three other women who, I discovered, were new recruits.

I was summoned to the Training Major's office. He seemed to come from the same spiteful mould as the Captain at Guildford. His first words to me as I entered his office were, 'Corporal George, you're back in the real world now! You will go through basic training again and pass out with the recruits. Understood?'

I was furious. 'No!' I replied, 'I did my basic training eight years ago.'

The Major stood up and gave me his opinion of the Det. 'From what I have seen of your unit, you're all slovenly, wholly self-opinionated and in need of discipline.' With that I was dismissed.

My roommates hardly spoke to me at all. When they did, they stood to attention and were obviously frightened of me. Later on they told me that they thought I was a spy put there by Second Lieutenant Andrews, the female officer in charge of new recruits. My actions over the first few days convinced them otherwise. I decided to make the best of a bad job and made myself at home in the room with the other three girls. Whilst they had sheets on their beds and ironed their blankets with the regulation crease down the centre as did all the recruits, I preferred a quilt.

The first morning of the course I found I was not the only NCO attending. There were six others, all men and all from different regiments and backgrounds. I suppose there was a small comfort to be had from this. At least I was not being made to go 'back to basics' just because I was a woman.

During NAAFI break that first morning one of my roommates came up to me and said politely, 'Excuse me, Corporal.

Lieutenant Andrews wants a word with you in the block.' I followed her back to our room where Lieutenant Andrews was waiting. She was a very young officer, almost certainly still in her teens and probably on her first posting. She was also overweight and untidy. Her white shirt had been carelessly ironed and had 'tramlines' down the sleeves; her shoes were scuffed and had not been polished in a long time. She stood, her arms folded. At her feet was my quilt, which had been pulled off my bed and lay in a heap on the floor. 'What's this, Corporal?' she enquired, pointing to the quilt. 'It's a quilt,' I said, stating the obvious. 'Don't get smart with me, Corporal. From now on I expect you to bed block every morning.' Something inside me snapped and, staring straight into her face, I exploded,

'I don't know who the hell you think you are, but don't you ever strip my bed again. Look at you. You're a disgrace!' She blanched and backed out of the room. There was an uneasy silence, broken only by the sound of my roommate pulling my quilt back on to the bed. 'Do all corporals talk to officers like that?' she asked timidly. 'No. Only if they've got a death wish,' I muttered.

The course continued but I found myself becoming more and more resentful of the way I had been treated.

One evening I was sitting in the Mess watching the news. On to the television screen flashed a picture of a soldier in plain clothes, waving a pistol over his head. He was surrounded by an angry mob. I heard myself crying out as I rocked forward, feeling sick. The soldier was Derek. Our paths had crossed many times, as he had worked in Northern Ireland with the Royal Signals for many years and was a genuinely nice man. It later transpired that he was about to leave the province and was showing his replacement around when he had got lost. The news reporter explained that he and his companion had been captured and killed in Belfast after being trapped by the angry mob, who were attending an IRA funeral. There had been a film crew reporting the funeral and their cameras had kept rolling. I watched in horror as the report showed in all its grisly detail the deaths of the two young men. Then I held my head in my hands and sobbed. How I hated the cameraman who had treated this human tragedy as nothing more than a news item.

Derek's death was the final straw. I knew that I could no longer stay in the Army. I had put an end to this futile existence. There was a three-day exercise coming up and I decided to complete it and then resign.

The exercise began with us being divided into groups. We were dropped on a country lane at night and told to march to the campsite that had been set up in a wood. We had a young lad in charge of us and he had made a good job of organizing the camp. Once we had reached the camp we were told to recce a copse two miles away and to report on the enemy strength.

Five of us wandered off towards the copse. The young lad in charge said that we must stick to the route given to him by the Directing Staff: on no account were we to deviate from this route as certain areas were out of bounds. This did not sound right to me and I took the lad to one side and explained that in a real life situation there are no areas that are out of bounds. It was obvious that the DS were expecting our group to fail in the task we had been set. They had made failure a certainty, as the route the lad had been given took us over open fields on a night bright with moonlight. Leaving the other three recruits at the rendezvous the lad and I crept along a sheltered track and into the copse.

Around a fire sat the DS. There were four of them, one of whom was Lieutenant Andrews. Parked to one side was a Land Rover. Lieutenant Andrews was laughing about something. None of them knew that they were being watched. Then a sergeant looked at his watch and said, 'Well, I think it's about time to sort out those sprogs now. They should just about be coming up over the hill.' 'Pathetic, aren't they Sergeant?' Lieutenant Andrews sneered. They all laughed and stood up, noisily making their way out of view. I waited until they had gone and then crept forward and let down the tyres of the Land Rover. The lad was amazed and asked if I was allowed to do that. I told him that I most certainly was!

We moved quickly back to where the other three were waiting for us at a road junction and headed back to camp. We then radioed in to the base to tell them that the enemy was four in strength and that they had transport. The Sergeant at the other end of the radio was only interested in finding out if we knew anything about the Land Rover being disabled. I denied all knowledge of it.

During that night and for the next two days the camp was attacked and we had to retreat. The recruits were all worn out from the lack of sleep and the constant attacks.

The last morning of the exercise dawned crisp and clear. All the sections had been reunited and we formed a group of about thirty. We were briefed by a sergeant to attack a wood which was ahead of us, beyond a sheep fence. We lay on the ground waiting for the signal to attack. As the flare went up we ran forward in a line. I cleared the fence and went on into the gloom of the wood. I bent down and watched the recruits as they ran forward, totally out of control but obviously enjoying themselves. Then the training corporals and sergeants emerged out of the darkness, firing blank rounds close to the heads of the recruits and pushing and kicking them. I stood up and ran towards one corporal who had knocked a recruit to the ground and was standing over him, kicking him in the side. Without a thought I rammed my SMG into the corporal and, as he doubled up, smashed the butt into his face. One of the other NCOs on the course had seen what had happened and he ran to my side yelling at the prostrate corporal, 'Enjoy kicking kids, do ya? Well have some of this,' and he kicked the corporal in the side. A training sergeant rushed up and I levelled my SMG at his face. 'What a hero! Young kids the best you can do?' I asked him.

The whole thing sickened me. These people were little more than thugs, hiding behind their uniforms. The recruits they were terrorizing were in the Intelligence Corps and it was not a front-line unit. They had no need of training like this to enable them to collate information. It was apparent that the training staff had no guts, otherwise they might have volunteered to do something useful in Northern Ireland themselves.

I went back to camp and immediately wrote out my letter of resignation. I took it directly to Lieutenant Andrews and threw it on her desk. Without waiting for a reaction I walked out. Within hours I was called to the Training Major's office. He had my letter in front of him and agreed that I could leave. He countersigned my report and that was it. I was taken off the course and after ten days' kicking my heels I drove out of the barracks as a civilian.

EPILOGUE

I was relieved to be out of the Army, but now had another problem. What was I going to do? The only ambition I had ever had was to be in the Army. I looked at the little red book I had been given when I left. What was I trained to do? Close-quarter combat and house assaults, just what a prospective employer wanted to see; such useful attributes to have in an office!

Back home I went to the job centre and registered with a number of employment agencies. The reality of my situation was depressing. I discovered that modern offices used computers far in advance of anything that the Army had. Although I had been trained to operate pull cord switchboards these had long since been replaced with computerized facilities, everywhere, that is, except in the Army. Eventually I managed to get a filing job in a local factory. It was a small unit and the noise of the machinery was unbearable. I hated it from the moment I walked through the door and walked out at the end of the first day.

Then one day I received a phone call from one of the SAS lads that I had known in Ireland. He told me about a company in London which was looking for ex-soldiers either from the SAS or from 14 Company to do surveillance work or to act as bodyguards. I telephoned the company and made an appointment to speak to someone at their office in Kensington. I found that it was a professional outfit working all over the world. It was rumoured to be government-sponsored but it was also said that they would deny any involvement should things go wrong.

I attended the meeting and was offered a contract on the spot. The wages were incredible. I earned £60 per day plus expenses and a petrol allowance if I had to use my own car. At that time it was a small fortune. I worked for them for a year doing various jobs all over the country. I even received an offer to go out to the Middle East and act as bodyguard to a member of the Saudi Arabian royal family. There were other offers from rich Arab families and an opportunity to work in an African country with some of my former colleagues from Northern Ireland. I was tempted by the offers but, by now, Peter had returned from his tour in Belize and had been posted back to Northern Ireland. I wanted something more permanent and so I decided to leave.

Peter and I were married in 1989 and I settled down in my home town and began working for the local County Council. Peter was still in the army in Northern Ireland. Life remained difficult for us as we spent so much time apart. After a couple of years we gave up the struggle and parted, eventually divorcing.

It has taken me ten years to get around to telling my story.

For much of that time I have been trying to recover from the military experience. I spent a lot of time being angry at the way we were treated over in Northern Ireland. It is true that we were volunteers, but those under whose jurisdiction we came had a very cavalier attitude towards us and our wellbeing. Although they were satisfied when things went well they would have had no hesitation in sacrificing any one of us had they believed it would further their cause. I think that the bitterness I felt towards the Special Branch of the RUC will remain with me always. Those police officers played with our lives with total indifference and many of them were no better than the terrorists they were supposed to be fighting.

Stress was unheard of within military circles in the 1980s, although its effects were well known elsewhere. None of us was offered any counselling or therapy to help us through the traumatic events in which we had been involved. Many of the soldiers engaged in covert work in Northern Ireland paid a heavy price for the privilege of defending Queen and country. Our only means of dealing with the pressure was to drink to excess. That in itself created more problems. Many of the men admitted to having beaten their wives because they were unable to understand what they were going through and many marriages were wrecked by the kind of lives they had to lead. One of the support staff, who was known to me, committed suicide because he was unable to cope with the pressure.

The Det worked well on a day-to-day basis because rank was not an issue. We each performed the tasks for which we were best suited, a situation unheard of elsewhere. During the time I was in the Army officers came from the privileged classes. They were the graduates of grammar or private schools; very few officers had a secondary school education. The Army rarely promoted from the rank and file. Experienced NCOs remained at sergeant or warrant officer level while being commanded by officers serving three-year commissions before going on to jobs in the City. Very few officers commanded respect from those beneath them, mainly because they treated them as inferior beings. Many would not even speak to other ranks, preferring to address their remarks through NCOs. There were of course some officers who treated other ranks as individuals and encouraged them to progress, but they were in a minority. One such officer was Major T and I shall always be grateful to her for the help that she gave me.

Since we now live in a time of more openness and equality, I hope that the Army has reflected this change and has become more open in its methods of selecting and dealing with people. Since women are now being allowed to join regiments that were once male preserves it seems as if it might now be keeping pace with the rest of society. I hope so, as this surely can be the only way forward.

Ten years on, the problems in Northern Ireland remain. I realize that when I went to serve there, full of hope for the future, I was expecting a miracle. In spite of the army presence, the talks, the cease-fires, even the Good Friday, 1998, agreement, the shootings and bombings have not stopped. Innocent people are still being killed and maimed and will continue to be while the men of violence are allowed to terrorize the peaceful majority.

On 23 May, 1998, a referendum was held in Ireland on whether or not to adopt the Good Friday agreement. Most commentators agreed that a spirit of compromise would be needed if peace were to be achieved. The result of the referendum was overwhelmingly in favour of the agreement. The following day there was a news report on television about the result of the referendum and the way in which it would affect the lives of the people of Ulster. An interviewer had gone to a Loyalist area of Belfast and had asked a woman there what she thought of the result. She looked around her and then said, 'We, here, are Orangemen. We don't need to compromise.'

When there are still people in Northern Ireland with such ignorant and confrontational views I wonder if there will ever be peace in that troubled land.

No doubt the woman was thinking of the atrocities committed by the IRA when she spoke and it is true that there have been many. What this woman had not considered, however, was the way in which Catholics have been treated by her people in years gone by. There is no doubt that they have been regarded as second-class citizens. The RUC were brutal in their attempts to crush them and it was they who lost control of the situation and asked the British Government for help in regaining the upper hand.

The IRA and other terrorist groups have killed many soldiers, police and innocent civilians both in Ireland and on the United Kingdom mainland. The Army and Police in turn have killed many terrorists and innocent people who got in their way. Now, as the twentieth century draws to a close, both sides are at last sitting down and talking to each other. I hope that the men of violence, both Catholic and Protestant, can at last accept the will of the people and give up their weapons.